MW00877296

Studio Life

Rob Easterla

ARCHWAY
PUBLISHING

Copyright © 2020 Rob Easterla.

All rights reserved. No part of this book may be used or reproduced by any means,
graphic, electronic, or mechanical, including photocopying, recording, taping or
by any information storage retrieval system without the written permission of the
author except in the case of brief quotations embodied in critical articles and reviews.

This book is a work of non-fiction. Unless otherwise noted, the author
and the publisher make no explicit guarantees as to the accuracy of
the information contained in this book and in some cases, names of
people and places have been altered to protect their privacy.

Archway Publishing books may be ordered through booksellers or by contacting:

Archway Publishing
1663 Liberty Drive
Bloomington, IN 47403
www.archwaypublishing.com
844-669-3957

Because of the dynamic nature of the Internet, any web addresses or
links contained in this book may have changed since publication and
may no longer be valid. The views expressed in this work are solely those
of the author and do not necessarily reflect the views of the publisher,
and the publisher hereby disclaims any responsibility for them.

Any people depicted in stock imagery provided by Getty Images are
models, and such images are being used for illustrative purposes only.
Certain stock imagery © Getty Images.

ISBN: 978-1-4808-9139-5 (sc)
ISBN: 978-1-4808-9141-8 (hc)
ISBN: 978-1-4808-9140-1 (e)

Library of Congress Control Number: 2020909337

Print information available on the last page.

Archway Publishing rev. date: 11/09/2020

For
Penny Nickels
of Fort Wayne, Indiana

and

Schaun Belston
of Powell, Wyoming

Contents

I was 7 years old in the summer of 1970 and thrilled to be learning risqué dance numbers from my Aunt Terri, 15, who I was visiting in Las Vegas, Nevada. She introduced me to this pre-war chestnut:

> *I'm a little teapot, short and stout*
> *Here is my handle, here is my spout*
> *When I get all steamed up, then I shout*
> *Sock it to me baby, let it all hang out!*

I knew the last line, borrowed from TV's "Laugh-In" was somewhat sexual, whatever that meant. Aunt Terri enhanced the routine by encouraging me to growl the last line, isolating my hips in a circular motion and ending with a giant forward bump. My arms were fashioned like a teapot handle and a teapot spout, until both hands went behind my head for the big bump finish.

Naturally, upon returning to school in the fall, I could think of nothing better than the teapot number, for the 1st – 4th Grade Talent Show. The number got huge laughs in Vegas at family functions and I was prepared to kick it up a notch with a costume. I cut strips of cardboard and painted them with bright orange tempera paint. I curved the cardboard panels from my neck to my waist, turning my body into a large orange orb. I finished the look with a teapot lid/hat that did not move, thanks to a thick elastic band under my chin and several staples. The lid/hat was worn at an angle and obscuring one eye to give the act mystery and depth.

I sauntered around backstage giving all the nervous kids winks and finger guns, grinning through thinly veiled chuckles at those who thought they had a chance: a dog act, mimes, cart-wheelers—as if.

Then, in walked Bobby Teller. Bobby was dressed like a grown up, or one of those tweens on the cover of Tiger Beat magazine. He had purposefully poured splotches of bleach all over his new jeans and wore a blousy shirt, unbuttoned to his navel. "Hey, Bobby," I said casually, "so, what's your act?"

"Just some song from the radio," he shrugged as he blew his hair dry into two magnificent blonde wings. "Oh, well, good luck," I tossed.

'Of course! How could I have been so stupid?! This is third *grade! Teapots are out! Pop stars are in!!'* I wanted to die, straining to remember lyrics to "I'm a Believer". A 6th Grader with a clipboard approached Bobby Teller. "You're up first," he said to Bobby. Bobby nodded professionally and started gyrating his body off-stage, getting in the mood, and worked his way in from stage right, to a thumping backbeat of "Sugar, Sugar" by The Archies.

> *"Sugar, ah honey honey*
> *You are my candy girl*
> *And you got me wanting you..."*

Girls of all ages shoved their way to the front row, screaming and fainting in waves.

I held out my good arm—the handle—to stop 6th Grader With the Clipboard from coming any closer as he pranced toward me. My eyes narrowed. "Lemme guess," I hissed. "I'm up next." I would have to *follow* Bobby Teller!

I crept onto the stage amid smirks and faces full of question marks. Acapella, I began. At the end of my act there was only silence. Humiliated, I looked down at my ratty tennis shoes. And then, like a tsunami, I felt the air being pulled away from me, only to come crashing back with applause like thunder. I had never felt that before, and only a handful of times since. My friend Chris Holden says 'it's the thrill of people appreciating your work, who don't even know you. They are reacting to some sort of talent'. And so began my love affair with show business.

At 18, I was meandering by various audition postings in Foley Hall at school. One Vietnam drama casting caught my eye that advertised for a "teen-aged white boy." I was summoned to an audition that night, reporting to somewhere in downtown Los Angeles. The audition was for a reading of a new play.

I arrived at the apartment of director Edmund Cambridge where a group of people he had assembled, looked on.

Although it was my first time acting with a black company, I felt I knew exactly what I was in for. When it comes to acting I knew, these people are not kiddin' around.

"AT RISE…" it began, and off we went, in it to win it. There was yelling—lots of contractions, there was crying, there was forehead-to-forehead physicality. I was at once terrified and riveted.

I think I got the part because I was the only guy who looked younger than 40. We performed the piece as a reading downtown at a space called "Crossroads". I was 18 and my character—the only whitey *near* the production, had a scary monologue which he spoke to his best friend, while standing on a land mine. Both he and his friend knew my character would die the moment my character shifted his weight. This became a common device among Nam scribes in the 80s. Those monologues, popular and abundant as they may have been, must always be performed from way down deep. You must plant your feet like tree roots and the sounds of your words come from a weird, uncomfortable place. If you're the least bit tentative or unsure, the words will be laughable. I learned that by watching the best. When Blair Underwood or Denzel, or Madge Sinclair or Lynne Thigpen growl deathly speeches, you know they are not playing games. When it's real, and not necessarily perfect, everyone feels it.

I was in over my head and our director, Ed, knew it. He called a special rehearsal where he had me close my eyes and slowly turn in circles, arms out like a gentle helicopter, to lose any sense of self and editorial stupidity, repeating the monologue over and over. We got closer to the truth that day but it still wasn't great. Ed had a booming voice like James Earl Jones and I was afraid of him. He sent me home, both of us unhappy, and I felt terrible.

Show day came and there I was, in a small auditorium packed with an audience who expected intense acting, for sure. When the big monologue came, I went to the terror place Ed had shown me, and my own terror place, being in an unknown urban setting.

They lined up! The audience lined up after the show to congratulate me! And I do mean "lined up"! It was like a dreamy wedding party reception line, of actors I had seen in movies and on TV, from big hits like "Sanford and Son" and "Sounder". I felt their presence meant they were telling the truth! It doesn't get any better than that. I was sort of crying as I shook their hands and I was overwhelmed by their kindness. I was a dopey kid from Oregon and they were all pros and they didn't have to be nice to me. Ed had absolutely scared that performance out of me, and I thank him for that experience. Whatever works! If the bitch can't get it, slap him around and scare him until he does! Ed knew I was intimidated by my fellow actors and the crowd, and he used that to scare me and he knew I was scared. It would come to be my proudest acting moment. It is perhaps my favorite acting experience because, like the third grade talent show, I had moved a whole roomful of people.

New to the Los Angeles basin, dear friend Peter Murphy and I wrangled a pair of invites to our first official production wrap party. This one was at the home of the immensely popular Mariette Hartley, also one of the picture's stars.

Upon entry, Peter and I passed by the hilariously British production secretary "Angela" who noticed Peter and I were both donning alligator-crested Izod shirts—our uniform in 1982, of Crème de Mint and Hunter Green. "You boys must have the same tailor," Angela quipped.

The San Fernando Valley, Hartley home was beautiful. A mostly outdoor party on a perfectly balmy night, guests enjoyed the secluded multi-level property, presenting tennis courts, a swimming pool and a Mariachi band.

After one beer I spotted Jodie Foster. After three beers I sauntered up to Ms. Foster, coolly, I thought. Her eyes searched for a casual escape route upon my boorish approach, but I had her cornered. We had Loyola Marymount University in common where I was a Soph and her friend Katherine was also a student. I crushed my empty beer can with one big, strong hand and blurted something vulgar that I cannot remember. She probably became a lesbian at that moment.

Meanwhile, Peter, deep into beer 4, had cooked up a frat-like plan to turn this expensive and tasteful gathering into a real Hollywood party! "Ya see Ed Asner up there, talking to those two big dumb jocks by the pool?" Peter asked.

In 1982, Mr. Asner was riding a formidable wave of fame after creating the character Lou Grant on the CBS summer surprise "The Mary Tyler Moore Show", one of the best shows in television history. A stocky man with immense forearms and broom-curled eyebrows that expressed a million emotions, Asner was beautifully put together. The public loved his crusty but benign demeanor and Ed was having a love affair with the world. Throw in appearances in landmark events "Rich Man, Poor Man", "Roots" and the MTM spin-off "The Lou Grant Show" and you got yourself a great big star.

"Here's the plan!" Peter whisp-slurred: "We ambush Ed and push him in the pool!" As Peter and I jogged toward Ed, the band played a particularly peppy Spanish tune, like a silent movie accompaniment to our steeple chase. We darted up the hill, hurdling hedges, bobbing and weaving as 19 year-old boys do. Ed's jock bodyguards wore Izods too, of course: Dusty Rose and Midnight Blue. Changing from gazelles to rhinos, Peter and I leapt in unison, and pushed poor Ed right into the deep end.

Peter and I had visited the set of this particular movie production earlier that summer, and had said perhaps 5 words to Ed, so I am positive he had no idea who we were.

Ed rolled himself out of the water, onto the pool's edge. Dusty Rose and Midnight Blue pushed me and Peter into the Hartley pool and all of us gasped our way out. We clawed our way toward the house for some reason, barreling through a blur of musicians, brass instruments and black velvet waist coats. We did not stop at the door-- oh, no— instead, being chased by Dusty Rose and Midnight Blue, we ran circles through every room of the house which was cheerfully decorated, but now awash in chlorinated pool water. We four drenched Izods ducked into a guest room, only to find—you guessed it—Jodie Foster, having a normal grown-up conversation with three gal pals. They said nothing, but really said everything with their slack jawed looks of disgust.

We were summoned to the living room by Mariette where beloved American icon Ed Asner stood, soaked.

"May I dry those things for you?" our hostess offered, graciously, praying we would just leave. "Naaaw", we replied, thinking it was good manners to save her the work.

Mariette had an extraordinary seashell collection she had tastefully displayed on a long narrow table, behind the back of her couch. Also, her bold, black and white foyer floor remained in my mind until I could copy those motifs later in my own home! So, all was not lost in our jaunty round of "Tag! You're Dead." I had discovered two hot new decorating ideas! Ed would only shake his fist at us, and from a distance.

I wrote my senior thesis paper on playwright Edward Albee. I've read every syllable he's ever published. Albee's "Who's Afraid of Virginia Woolfe" is the greatest American play ever written. I had high hopes for Albee's "The Goat or Who is Sylvia?", and, sure enough, I think it's probably the second greatest American play ever written.

I saw one of Albee's "The Goat..." actors, Eddie Redmayne, in Piccadilly, London after the show. I grabbed him tightly and he was smart enough to realize aloud: "OH! I guess you just saw the show,'" as he pried my sobby cheek from his temple. I wanted to eat him up but I'm pretty sure it's against the law in England.

It cannot be expressed, the ecstasy/vomitous feeling I was teeter-tottering, after sneaking into an audition Albee held in Southern California for two new one-act plays he had written and was casting.

Albee was short and a concentrated powerhouse of terrifying passion but flashed me an "It's going to be OK" smile when I entered the theatre. He trotted from the stage to the back of the house where I waited, quaking, and he shook my hand. His hands were not large but his fingers were thick and warm and feeling his hand in mine, I almost collapsed and fainted. He had brown, shaggy, shoulder-length hair and he was tired, probably from seeing half-assed actors all day.

I had rehearsed to death a monologue from Peter Schaffer's "Five Finger Exercise". I spoke it directly to my character's father whom I placed, seated, in a chair, down stage left.

Edward quietly said, "Go ahead."

Just as my desperate yelling at the empty chair began to feel awkward, Edward yelled "Stop!" He said, "Take it from the top and *never* put another character or chair on stage with you during an audition monologue. Deliver it to *us*—the audience is the other character. That is a note I never forgot, and I employed it many times after. Amazing how a few minutes in the presence of greatness can change everything.

Albee took the time to work with me and he changed my approach a few more times. Despite the things I read of him being crabby and curmudgeonly, I only think of him as a man who took the time to help me. He was brusque and quick and demanding but he made me a better actor in twenty minutes time! It was one of the greatest gifts ever given to me.

I didn't get the part but I left that day on a cloud, adoring him even more than I had. They say you should never meet your heroes, but I'm so glad I did.

Established over a hundred years ago, movie studios in and around Hollywood, California, still present themselves with a utilitarian modesty, despite the star-spangled hype of their own publicity machine. For employees who can stay out of trouble, studio life offers a simple, straightforward existence, overflowing with all the tangible qualities of small town America. Bicycles float cheerful worker bees to the mill and the mailroom. At lunchtime, carpenters and secretaries unite, chatting their way down tributaries to the commissary, where table-hopping percolates between studio hairdressers and studio brass.

A testament to successful evolution, life on the lot, to the casual observer, is a work-a-day world that embraces an American ideal, when the twentieth century was new. Guarded and gated still, dream factory communities carry their own torch, paying tribute to humble but spectacular beginnings. The traditions of an era are preserved to commemorate the halcyon days when movies were born.

Actress Faye Dunaway stammered it best in 1987, when asked to describe her first day on the Paramount lot: "… I remember you feel-- it's just exciting, it's just, you feel it's glam--, it's, it's where everything happened so long ago, you know? And it's still here just as it was."

Early film companies were created by European immigrants, American dreamers, and veterans of the Great War. The movie pioneer talent pool appeared to be a haphazard convergence, but they shared a commonality as survivors, and adventurers in their way. Founding fathers were ruthless in business, and they were gamblers, taking risks against all odds. Their gambling was honest, conflicted as that concept may seem. Time has revealed them to be bombastic men, egocentric and manipulative, but human, nonetheless. However fraught with human frailties, and because their frailties were human, the movies were borne out of human innocence. Today, movies are fueled by innocence lost.

When movie people put a "spin" on something, it's what normal people call a "lie". We've even put a spin on our own work environment. We happen to enjoy facades. Is that so wrong?

The picture of a small factory town is a brave mask. Inside the charming stucco bungalows, studio wizards face a willful tempest. Once enjoying a sunny romp through the citrus groves of Southern California, the motion picture business is no longer a carefree child. All grown up, Hollywood studios have become imprisoned by their own business models that may hinge, ironically, on the child-like sense of creativity they struggle to re-capture. As the studio giant grows, so does the potential for cataclysm, and also the potential for enormous success and global notoriety.

To be part of a hit movie is to know the thrill of victory. Spoils to the victor as box office coffers are dumped directly into studio pockets, and our world is swimming in cash. The Monday following a successful opening weekend discovers the lot staffed only with creative geniuses. A unique sensation that is felt by the entire world outside our gated enterprise, a hit movie has defined those of us inside the gates as purveyors of popular culture and it is sheer stardom. Gambling and striking it rich, echoes our forebears. It is the American dream, realized.

When times are tough, there is a certain prowess and an inherent showmanship among studio employees. We take pride in hiding the cracks. Sometimes through clenched teeth, we find it important to uphold the ideology that sustains us, with hope and optimism and a "can-do" sense of pride. Studio folk are thick-skinned and truly fearless at times. Real bravery peppered with false bravado and a sense of humor is, after all, the American way.

Making movies is the singular American art form. While the rest of the world claims everything from music to cuisine, Americans can hold their head high, claiming movies as our single, but large, contribution to world culture. Filmmaking is not only American, but more specifically, Californian. Stan from Burbank runs the Grip Dept. Sue from Santa Monica keeps inventory for Wardrobe, and Rob, who now lives just around the corner, sorts the fan mail for Publicity. This is where I come in to my studio life, galloping up Windsor Avenue onto the Paramount Pictures lot in 1985, cheerfully and much too eager.

Like Faye Dunaway and me, portrait photographer John Engstead tells about his first day at Paramount in his book *Star Shots*. He describes it as a chaotic benchmark, when, at that moment in 1926, the Publicity Dept. was scrambling to promote—I mean, cover-- the death of their own Rudolph Valentino. My first days at Paramount were marked by more hopeful circumstances: wrapping principle photography on a picture called "Top Gun". A romantic homage to patriotism, no one could predict that the world would have a need—the need for speed. For leading lady Kelly McGillis it would mean a high-profile film career that she would use as a springboard for a formidable life in the theatre. And for star Tom Cruise and director Tony Scott, "Top Gun" would forever cement them into Hollywood's upper echelon of big boy players.

Shooting interiors for "Top Gun" appeared on call sheets during my first week at the studio. I crept by the sound stages, painfully aware of the revolving red light, spinning above the stage door, warning passers-by that cameras were turning. Tony Scott would have appreciated my obsequious tiptoe then, particularly because I would burst onto his "Beverly Hills Cop II" shooting stage two years later, despite the red light warning.

But that's another story...

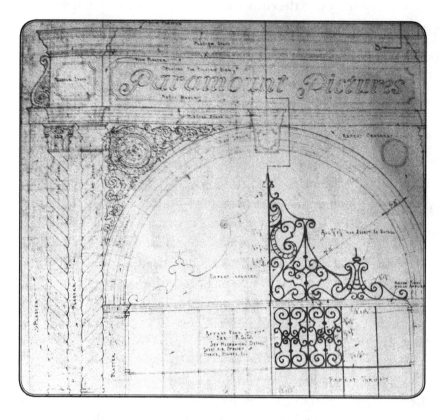

Detail from the original Paramount Pictures Bronson Gate blueprint designed in 1926.

As one of Paramount Marketing's numerous support staff, I used the catered press conference for "Beverly Hills Cop II", as a means of feeding myself lunch.

My argyle sweater vest and Brigitte Nielsen's shoulder had met several weeks earlier when she and I, both of us unflinching upon approach, had collided as we crossed paths on a narrow thoroughfare under scaffolding that outlined the Zukor Bldg. construction site. Ms. Nielsen was a leading player on "Cop II" and undoubtedly thrilled to be sharing a billing block with Eddie Murphy, Paramount's favorite son. An adored and staunch member of the Paramount family, Eddie was revered with unconditional love, despite the garish "Eddie Murphy" signature, forged in sizzling neon above his office door, and the maroon pom-poms that swung from the top-liner of his golf cart.

On this very special day, "Cop II's" director Tony Scott, and his stars Eddie and Brigitte were taking a break from shooting to field questions from the press in a corner of their shooting stage. Fifty or so journalists were corralled onto Stage 12 where a little dais was erected before some folding chairs. The periphery was festooned in turkey platters, coffee and crudité.

Publicist Allison Jackson had returned to our office early from the press conference. In those days, Allison was intimidating and driven. She later calmed down and became a really nice person! Looking back, that transformation was foreshadowed when she breezed by my desk with good will, suggesting I "go over for some lunch before the reporters get it all". There was not a trace of entrapment or irony that I could detect. "Will do!" I chirped. I was sorting fan mail that afternoon, alphabetically, and set "Fonda, Jane" as my stopping point.

At 3:45, having lost all track of time, I set out for Stage 12. Perhaps Eddie Murphy would embarrass me, I fantasized, by waving hello across the footlights, prompting reporters to ask who his little friend was. Eddie and I had given each other the cursory studio nod from passing golf carts, after all. He may recognize me and give me a shout out. And would Brigitte's shoulder remember my sweater vest? She may shake her fist at me jokingly, so I prepared some clever quips for the press, should she spot me.

A line had formed at the south side of Stage 12 where those wanting entry, waited patiently. I, very officiously scooted my way past the goofy novice drones. Apparent by their gasps and tugs at my clothing, they didn't know who I was, and how they were painfully unaware of my carte blanche status. 'They don't get it', I thought, smugly: 'The spinning red light is because of our press conference.' I reached the top of the stair and lunged for the door. A large man at the front of the line stood in my way, thrusting his forearm in front of me. "They're rolling!" he warned. "Puh-leeze", I countered, and grasped the long door handle that looked like it might be attached to a meat locker. With both hands, I engaged in a slow and steady pull. Satisfied with my strength, the thick vault door yawned open and I sauntered in.

I strolled 20 feet into the darkness, slowing to a crawl before I stopped to let my eyes adjust. Suddenly I was standing in an adobe village, somewhere in New Mexico, it seemed. It was dusk and the sky was ripped with the orange and blue streaks of a gorgeous Southwest sunset. Eddie stood 15 feet from me. He raised his eyebrows in silence. It was not followed by his signature donkey bray guffaw or OK hand sign, or a golf cart wave. He was, however, wearing a leopard-print fez. Two men holding smoke machines stared at me, gaping, as my eyes followed the length of a camera crane, 20 feet up where Tony Scott was perched. His voice cracked through an electronic megaphone: "What's going on down there—who is that?" The cast and crew looked at me for an answer. I looked back at the doorway where I had entered. The large man who had tried to stop me shook his head as he slowly closed the coffin lid/door.

"I thought, the lunch, press… thing…" I fumbled, now light-headed and overcome with nausea and the realization of what I had done. Pride goeth before a fall, and I was making a swan dive straight into Grand Canyon. In my mind I began to chisel my escape through the cement floor of the sound stage. Charitably, a grip pointed me toward the opposite corner of the building.

"Thanks", I said, calmly. "Thank you… I appreciate it, so, ok…". I strode past Eddie and company in the direction I had been given. When I found my path blocked by set pieces, I began to crawl over some fiberglass rocks, climbing my way to the only channel I saw: the narrow space between the 50 ft. cyclorama backing and the soundstage wall. Cast and crew observed me silently, and with pity. I could barely fit through the teeny opening, eating asbestos as I clawed the length of the insulated wall. The New Mexico sky billowed unnaturally as the village fell under the attack of a 50 ft. nerd in a sweater vest. My monstrous shadow raced up the stage walls, stretching to the overhead catwalks with a menacing pitch and bounce.

I emerged on the other side of the cyclorama backing to find a short woman in a blue maid's outfit, working a silent carpet sweeper over the indoor/outdoor that had been laid down for the press. She looked at me carefully and with disdain, gesturing with a big eyeball-roll toward a tray of wilted lettuce and plastic picnic cutlery. Her helper stacked chairs, tsk-tsking me under his breath. Did I have the good sense to run out the door all the way to the Canadian border? No. In perfectly focused denial, I assembled a small sandwich from the fixin's that remained.

Hand in pocket and eyes darting from beam to beam overhead, I pantomimed for sweeper lady, some sort of purpose, indicating that I was completely recovered from my earlier faux pas and now needed to assess the ceilings, or something and get down to business. I finished my sandwich with dainty precision. Luckily there was a north-facing escape door that I then utilized.

Like a weirdo, once outside, I began to jog for no reason. One of my clammy hands clamped onto the top of my head as if to hold in the demons about to be exorcized. My hand slid down my face to my mouth, where it stayed for a minute, again, bottling the torment. I jog-trotted my way into the Marketing Dept. lobby where I dissolved into a guest chair. At that moment Greg Brinkley loped in and asked if I was ok. "Someone must be chopping onions", I answered, which I thought was clever. Greg is Christie Brinkley's brother, and like his sister, should automatically be a spokes-model for Pepsodent. Strange, how when you just need a smile, Hollywood sends in the best. Suit up, Brinkley!

Greg was shooting a movie on the lot called "She's Having a Baby". He was at my desk to use the lobby phone and chit-chat, and he was a welcomed distraction. Greg was off to the Hamptons that weekend so I was seething with envy. He had a funny story about what Kevin Bacon did on the set that morning. Allison Jackson drifted by with an annihilating comment; so savage that Greg and I clutched our sides laughing. Doug Collins popped his head around the corner and whispered that Sid Ganis just broke, into pieces his fourth telephone receiver that month. 'That is *so cool*", we agreed. We all yucked it up in the lobby for some time and the ol' gang had lifted my spirits.

The 1980s were a time when Hollywood still behaved like Hollywood. Wretched excess was the name of the game and at Paramount, we championed the call. Cocaine in the 80's is what Red Bull is to 2020: de reguere and omnipresent.

It was the chore of a colleague to procure hookers *and wardrobe* for said hookers, for a certain brassy production arm on the lot.

The 2-martini lunch was available and enforced at any number of restaurants all within a hundred yards of the studio gates. Oblatt's, Nickodell and Lucy's El Adobe-- always jumpin' with studio folk from our little movie colony. At Nickodell, the waitresses wore heavy eyeliner and delivered trays of liquor to every lunch table. We sat in a maze of high back red leather booths in a fog of cigarette smoke and martini glasses flying, until the party ended at around 2 pm. Then it was into the hot, blinding California sun where we plodded the sidewalk back to our Melrose gate. What reckless fun it was, but not without its own cathartic punishment in the end.

Every year, Paramount Human Resources threw a big company party, like a trip to a water slide park or a big boozy picnic somewhere. In 1987, the gift to all employees was the 75th Anniversary Party. The event was outdoors, on the lot, in the B Tank. Drained dry for the event, the B Tank was the ocean for every Paramount picture needing, well, an ocean. The giant backing on the B Tank, usually painted with stormy sea clouds had been painted white, like a giant drive-in movie screen.

Marie Varricchio and I arrived at the party on time, winding our way through giant portraits of Louise Brooks, Marlene Dietrich and Bob Hope. The B Tank was dotted with mini-sets and kiosk stations: the "Grease" diner, "The Godfather" pasta bar, and so on. The tents on the periphery, catering to caterers and staff were a city unto itself. Towering silver palm trees made of aluminum flanked the movie screen. It was a million dollar party and the stars came out for it. I enjoyed pot stickers with Sean Connery, and whined about studio politics with Michael J. Fox.

Frank Mancuso, our President of Production and CEO, took the stage. Under a magical summer sky, he presented two short films. The first was a tribute to Paramount's canon of movies by Chuck Workman and the second film was entitled "LIFE at Paramount". It had been produced only a few months earlier when LIFE magazine came to the lot for a 75th Anniversary daytime party on Stage 1. On that day, January 30, 1987, the usually unflappable studio folk crawled out of their ratty, pedestrian cubicles to join co-workers, hooting and hollering outside the Director's Bldg.

Fifty or more limousines had zig-zagged through the Melrose Gate, past the Dressing Room Bldg. and the Administration Bldg., to Stage 1 and the Bronson Gate. It is the very gate Gloria Swanson's Norma Desmond had breezed through, 37 years earlier in Billy Wilder's "Sunset Blvd." Limo doors opened at Stage 1, and out popped Gregory Peck, Jimmy Stewart, Janet Leigh, Olivia de Havilland and Burt Lancaster, and many more, alongside youngsters like Matthew Broderick, Deborah Winger and Timothy Hutton. It was a day of a hundred stars; Paramount's family of stars, who had come home to acknowledge their beginning, paying respect to that little plot of land where they had been reborn. It was, for Charles Bushinski, the *very* spot where he began-- the spot where he looked at the street sign outside the massive gate, and chose a new life as Charles "Bronson".

Well, I lost it. I made a nuisance of myself, breaking every rule of protocol and wallowing in a dream come true. In childhood, while my pals were playing baseball and inhaling fresh air, I was inhaling popcorn and sitting in the dark with these people. It can be tricky, as a kid, when your friends are merely a flicker of light and shadow. It turns out, they were real. It is no exaggeration to say, I could hardly believe I was walking among them and speaking to them.

One of the most lasting memories of that day was falling into Elizabeth Taylor's violet eyes. While I made stupid conversation with the teensy actress, I kept thinking she was possibly not human, because her eyes were an inhuman color. It was like swimming in violet pools. The experience was trippy and freaky and that's as articulate as I can be. I knew my near-nausea was the product of studio Publicity chiefs back in the day. The Publicity machine told us that Elizabeth Taylor was the pinnacle of beauty and stardom. Even with that knowledge to distance myself, and even through my own research, discovering her many sides including 'spoiled' and 'entitled', she was somehow nurturing, kind, funny and something special.

The nighttime party was winding down in the B Tank when I ran into my new pal Mike Wuetcher, alias "Wooch". Wooch, worked in the mailroom and little did he know his future at Paramount had just begun. He would become one of the studio's top publicists in the years ahead, after I left to begin my climb at Fox. For now, we were two drunken wobblers who didn't want to stand in line at the designated restrooms. We teetered our way in wide kooky-print neckties, Zodiak dress shoes and creased khaki's, to the dark and foreboding construction site of the Zukor Bldg.

On the periphery of the B Tank, the construction site was quiet and unlit, as we made our way through fresh earth and steel girders that would become the first floor Marketing suites, and for both of us, our new home. While urinating, we made a pact: If we were both still there in 25 years, at the studio's 100th Anniversary, we vowed to buy two revolvers, drive out to the desert and shoot each other in the head. We shook on it that night. And it almost happened. I bolted a few years later but Wooch created an empire until just before the Centennial in 2012. I think perhaps he fled his post, in an effort to dodge my swift bullet.

The first 75 years of fun and debauchery gave way to political correctness and appropriate behavior. One of our favorite, crabbiest and most bombastic producers overdosed and died. And many came close to death as that great pedigree of blowhard studio folk faced extinction. So many died at what they believed the studio wanted, or came so close to death, in Paramount's first 75 years. They were grist for the mill like the slaves of Pharaoh, says Paramount's own CB DeMille, when writing "The Ten Commandments" regarding the Jews in Egypt. Like the Jewish slaves, the studio giants left a legacy, never to be forgotten. Their blood was mortar for the bricks, used to build every soundstage.

My colleagues and I—Paramount staffers in the 1980s, received a gift beyond the 75th Anniversary party. It was not intended, but bequeathed to us anyway, as a message or anti-credo of sorts: Live large, keep the Hollywood myth alive for others, but don't let it kill you. Every generation is witness to the generation before them. For those of us willing to open our eyes, the lessons were not only clear, but screaming at us. How many lives will it take before we realize show biz can kill you directly, or at least take so much of your soul, only a vulnerable shell is left behind? Whether they were victims or overachievers or just wanted to shine, we must all respect John Balushi, River Phoenix, Joseph Mankiewicz, Don Simpson, Tony Scott, Debra Hill, Brendan Lee, Sharon Tate, Ed Hutson, Corey Haim, Judy Garland, Ned Tannen, Brad Grey and Bob Fosse, to name a few who decided to give themselves to their work, so that our world in the audience could be full of magic. It is a smarter Hollywood today for those of us who paid attention. Like Liza Minnelli says, "Give till it hurts." God rest their souls. And hats off to the incredible producer Bob Evans who has just died, but what a legacy he's left. Because of our colleagues who have passed, we have been given a brighter, better chance.

The 2-storey apartment at 6th and Cochran.
We decided I should paint a big head mural on the wall.
James Dean and me, 1985.

Studio life starts at home, and wouldn't any movie studio have *died* to corral what was happening at my apartment at 6th Street and Cochran Avenue?

I lived in the Miracle Mile District of Los Angeles at 603 S. Cochran, #301 with Robby Sella from 1985 to 1988. All the glamor that snap-crackle-popped in that home, came from Robby. He was a senior, after all, at UCLA where a frenzied talent pool swirled like a self-obsessed tornado, and egos flew like cattle and pick-up trucks. College pals since our frosh year at Loyola Marymount, Robby and I had planted the deep, dark seeds of show biz in each other, and wherever life has taken us, there is always a bumper crop to harvest. As our friend H. David C. Gunderman said, "I don't come over to watch TV. I come over to watch *you* two watch TV." As we sow, so shall we reap, and I must say, 1985 was a banner year with bushels and pecks for a lifetime.

We lived five blocks from Rexall Square—the mightiest and most beautiful of all the drug stores in the world. It is where Vincent Minnelli took little Liza, as a child, to buy pastel chalks and paper, to illustrate her problems away, and where Robby and I would browse hair dyes at 3am.

We often lunched at the Flying Saucer restaurant at Wilshire Blvd. and Cochran, originally built as The Wimpy Grill, with a 1930s pitched roof. It was razed in the '90s, replaced with a Staples. It was there we might find our ruggedly handsome landlord, George, dressed in normal clothes, despite his penchant for shorty silk kimonos which he wore when collecting rent checks.

We were separated only by the gorgeous affluence of Hancock Park from Paramount, our neighborhood dream factory. We enjoyed the spires of Pan Pacific Park from our rooftop where Robby and I lounged on slanted skylights planning tomorrow. We didn't know it then, but our life was a dreamy wonderland, the way all kids live in a dreamy wonderland today and don't know it. Who is to say if it was real or just enhanced by time? I've decided, because it was real to us, then it's real forever.

The Miracle Mile neighborhood was then, just as it is today. The energy of the people is purely creative. I was studying acting then, and we, the actors and writers and directors and 3-ring circus jugglers, were all happily stuck with each other. Lee Wilkoff, fresh off his stint in "Little Shop of Horrors" moved in on Cochran, just north of us. I didn't know him, but I stalked him from the comfort of my bed on the 4th floor where I watched the entire neighborhood search for their cars, haphazardly parked on 6th St., the night before.

Our pal Jason Ma delighted audiences every night at the Shubert Theatre as Skimbleshanks in "Cats" while his handsome partner Ron Asher churned out plays from their Tudor upper on Cochran above 6th. Marie Varricchio barely had any home time on Detroit Ave., conquering the Equity Waiver scene as one of the most sought after stage managers in town. Marie's ex-boyfriend Dave Evans was about to sell his first script "Radio Flyer" for a million dollars as the result of a bidding war between Par and Warner Bros.

Dedicated actress Elinore O'Connell lived in a pink building on 6th and Cloverdale, and she envisioned herself playing one of the most beloved theatrical roles of our time, despite her lack of experience on the professional stage. We all knew El could sing the part. Ron called out of the blue one night to say Jason had been helping Elinore with her audition piece and Ron had crouched in the stairwell, listening. He said he got chills listening to her 16 bars. Although innocent looking, Ron Asher was a jaded realist and he never used "chills" to describe anything. So it was at once shocking and completely expected when our little Elinore stood in the audition line with everyone else in L.A. County at Highland and Franklin, and won the role she was after. We hadn't caught our breath by the time she appeared on the Tonight Show, and she was off and running, playing Fantine in "Les Miserables" at the Shubert, following Jason's star turn there in "Cats".

Dana Stevens was dating my Robby, and maybe she and I were competing for Robby. I don't think so, but who knows? We were similar people and fiercely competitive. Still, I couldn't get enough of Dana and we got on like a house on fire. A talented actress and playwright, Dana would go on to write successful screenplays and find herself half of quite a power couple, marrying the thoughtful and evocative movie director, Michael Apted.

One Thursday night when Robby was away, auditioning for regional theatre companies in Chicago, Dana became bored. She lived two blocks down on Detroit and asked if I wanted to go out. *"Do I?"*, I yelled. I had squirreled away a matchbook signed by the owner of the Imperial Gardens which meant free entry. The Imperial Gardens on Sunset was originally built as the Players Club. In 1986, on Thursday nights it was Boss Club! If you don't know what that means, I'm sorry for you. But I will tell you, every song the DJ played was Springsteen. And, baby, we were born to run.

Dana and I shoved onto the sweaty, low-ceiling dance floor, danced for 45 minutes and collapsed into a booth. I said, "Do you want to leave?" She said, "yes". She missed her Robby.

What fun it was, riding Robby's UCLA coattails, crashing parties at the UCLA-only "Pad o' Guys". The Pad was a real apartment in Westwood, which ran a river of hopeful boys through its strainer, always in search of the right members/tenants. The Guys were creepily elitist, a la 'Lord of the Flies' and writer/actor David Arnot was at the helm in 1986, screening applicants with a steely sense of humor. The Pad o' Guys churned out a monthly newsletter, after all, so tenants would have to live as four UCLA men with a certain amount of mystique and charisma, *and* be doing something with their lives to write about. It was a tough room.

Guys' Ed Soloman, Dana Stevens' ex-boyfriend, was an extremely nice person. I found his congeniality startling, given his notoriety as the youngest writer on ABC's primetime champion "Laverne &

Shirley". Ed could have been mean but he wasn't. Robby and I found Tim Robbins, more than once, shuffling about his simple but sublime Wallenboyd Theatre, downtown on the corner of Wall St. and Boyd St. I'm not kidding when I say he worked the lobby bare-foot, greeting audience members with his gorgeous mop of curls and winning interest in anyone who entered. Twenty-something and completely engaging, who cared if he was not wearing shoes?

It was a time of Elton and Barbra when they were beautifully cresting, making records hand over fist and coasting on their laurels. Madonna and Erasure were fixin' to explode, and Mariska Hargitay, a teeny UCLA student with long black hair and bangs, came over for scene study one night. The diminutive and handsome Thomas Calabro came for dinner before he became the scheming Michael on "Melrose Place".

Later, as Director, Photo Archive at Twentieth Century Fox, I would be in charge of preserving the images of Mariska Hargitay's mother, Jayne Mansfield, and of all the images associated with Dave Evan's script following "Radio Flyer", a film called "The Sand Lot" which Dave narrated himself. David Arnott's "Ford Fairlane" also fell under my jurisdiction, and what a sentimental pleasure it was, governing access to those properties.

Robby was accepted to the Juilliard School in New York in 1987, setting me adrift into the churning whirlpool of studio life. After Juilliard, Robby's first big break came when he was cast as Freddie in the Broadway revival of "My Fair Lady" and he would replace Alan Cumming as "Cabaret's" MC. Robby settled down with Tony nominee Enid Graham to play his best role as father to Valentino, Lorenzo and Gian Carlo. The boys are all really loud, and a bit like throwing yourself into a basket of puppies. Given their exceptional parents, I know that one day the boys will be given the opportunity to spread their wings however they see fit, as Robby and I had spread our wings atop the skylights at 6th and Cochran.

The majority of events that happened to me (or did I happen to them?) at Paramount were lessons in humility. I don't know why that is so, except to say I was in my mid-20s and predisposed to humiliation. My wordless moment with actor James Spader is a fine example.

Around 1987 I was occupying a cube for Exhibitor Services where nothing glamorous went on, however important, but statistical research. Who would have thought on this day, auditions for a big movie would be happening down the hall from me?

I had been working as a receptionist for Marketing, and one day at a weekend party hosted by a publicist, a woman approached me as I was lifting weights that had been scattered about, on a sun-drenched California redwood deck. Slathered in oil and benching 100, the glare of the sun was suddenly blocked by an attractive woman standing over me. She was new to Paramount-- a perky ray of light I had seen unboxing her possessions on our floor. "Aren't you our receptionist?" she asked. I confirmed, and with that she asked me to be her assistant.

The pretense of resumes and placement agencies and HR screenings is a joke. Oil up, lift some weights and they will come. That's how we do it in Tinsel Town and there is nothing wrong with that system. I was a good assistant!

So there I sat, in my beige cubicle in 1988, titter-tattering on the phone with a friend about a movie I saw the night before, starring James Spader.

"Well," I began, with one foot on my desk, pushing back beyond all expectations of a reclined position. "Do *not* get me wrong-- I love me some Jimmy Spader as much as the *next* guy, *but...*" I dug in with a sharp trowel: "Have you *seeeeen* 'Mannequin?" Then I blurted: "He is B. O. P. Yep, 'Box Office Poison.'"

As I mentioned, there were auditions going on down the hall from me. It seems they were reading for leading men that day in this little office space normally occupied by a marketing analyst.

I clenched my head down to my left clavicle, squeezing the phone-squishy attachment I had recently double stick-tapped to my receiver. Reveling now, in my own hilarious cruelty. I glanced left. There was a body sitting in a side chair that was usually unoccupied. I guessed it was an actor waiting for his audition/meeting down the hall. I guessed that since it was a Paramount feature film audition, it may be an actor of some renown. Guess who. Naturally, it was James Spader.

There he sat, smugly, as only Spader can smug. The King of Smug wore classic, original wire-rimmed aviator Ray-bans, dropping dangerously below his flopsy, sexy bed hair, as if to mock me. More so than when I ruined Eddie Murphy's take, and more so than dripping pool water over Jodie Foster, I fell apart inside. I have no idea what really happened next but I recall it in feelings and staggered emotional snapshots. I saw James, completely silent but with an ear-to-ear pencil-thin grin, just sitting and staring at me. Stars can be so very cruel. I don't know what happened to the telephone receiver, except that I babbled something into the mouthpiece and fake laughed and made a breathy, fraudulent buh-bye. I peeled my new phone squishy from my neck and put the receiver down, sort of in its cradle, maybe on my desk top. Then James was gone. Dear God, what had I done?

I do not dislike James Spader, nor do I believe he has *ever* been 'Box Office Poison'! In fact, his credits read like a who's who of popular filmmaking. I was being brash and stupid and I learned then, never throw strangers or anyone under the bus for a laugh, unless you mean it. And I did not mean it.

Since then I have been riveted to every project of which James is a part, including his soaring television career from "The Office" to "Boston Legal" and beyond. I am his biggest fan and no one will ever come between me and James. If he decides to perform "Phaedra" in a laundromat, I will be in the front row with fabric softener and a roll of quarters.

In 1988, I enjoyed a pivotal position, cubically that is, just west of the second floor elevators in Paramount's brand new Zukor Bldg. Clad in my omnipresent argyle sweater vest, white starched shirt and too-big-for-my-face Clark Kent glasses, I strode about the second floor with a regal air. I cared about everything then, from my Sperry Top-Siders to my immaculate desk.

My work station sported half-walls on one side, finished with teetery but workable counter plates, and thus became an airy and welcoming space for colleagues to relax and lean in. Although I was not a receptionist, many studio guests presumed I was, due to my half-walls and engaging personality, and I loved it.

Hammering away at my IBM Selectric typewriter one afternoon, my mind was swimming, almost in and out of consciousness, trying to make sense of the world. I had watched Ridley Scott's "Blade Runner" the night before and his arresting images along with the vile yet intoxicating storyline was jammin' my frequencies. Like a gallon of chocolate syrup, it made me sick and yet I couldn't get enough of it. While obsessing over every aspect of the film, including Sean Young's hairdo, I felt a chilly shadow come over my IBM Selectric. I turned quickly and followed the shadow, up, up, up with Replicant precision.

There, silhouetted by hideous fluorescent tube lighting was a "woman", 12 feet tall, framed by bouncy blonde curls and a beautiful smile. I could not believe it was Darryl Hannah, or should I say, Evil Replicant Blah-Blah Number What's-Her-Name? My hand to God, all I could think was, 'Do not eat me,' and 'do not kill me'. Poor Darryl, it seems was lost, and I stuttered some directions for her, good-naturedly. Remember, helpful stewardship is the studio way. We are ambassadors of good will, even when you think Darryl Hannah may gymnastics you to death. She had to duck to get into the elevator, and I fell face down into my IBM Selectric. The timing was unbelievable. I was never so scared, thanks to Ridley, Darryl and the power of movies.

A few weeks later a special day was upon us! Beloved co-worker, Pam, was celebrating a birthday, and it demanded the best of what we had to give: a big sheet cake, twenty minutes of innocuous banter, and champagne if you're lucky. Naturally, my workspace and environs was the designated hub for birthday celebrations, given my half-walls (a place for the cake) and tidy cubicle (looked good in pictures).

Preparation began at 2:30 as Leslie and Linda slowly sidestepped the cake into place. Leslie and Linda were both smart, pretty, had girly voices and had been sorority sisters at USC. They both worked in Marketing Accounting, and both extremely corporate. I loved them. They were *on it* at 2:30. By 2:45 the area around my cubicle was brimming with Marketing personnel. The smell of fresh coffee filled the air, and what a beautiful sight: little plastic cups and forks, napkins fanned, adroitly, a big white cake wishing Pam the very best and next to the cake, a large, gleaming butcher knife exactly like the knife from the shower scene in "Psycho". The light bounced off the blade, flashing at me.

> 2:58: The crowd has grown to about 40 hoverers. I laugh and kid, slapping hands away from the cake. The natives grow restless.

> 3:03: Pam, the guest of honor, bursts through double doors, colleagues pushing her, tee-heeing from behind. "*Whaaaaaat?*", her face seems to say as the crowd mosh-pits her to the cake. Pam is a gentle gal and she wears her hair in a mullet hairstyle. She is donning her usual work attire of creased dungarees and a plaid flannel shirt. (*Why* didn't we get it *sooner?*) She is pushed forward by the crowd and I ceremoniously hand her the murder weapon from the teetery cubicle half-wall shelf.

> 3:04: A screamy chorus of "Happy Birthday" cuts the air as Pam cuts into the cake.

3:05: Suddenly, Charline shoves her way through the crowd. Charline is a robust gal who works just a few cubicles down. She must be, I think, joining Pam in an hilarious "age thing" to help her blow out candles... or something.

3:05.3: My memory turns to a blurry, slow motion crime scene as Charline scoops half the cake into one massive paw and smears it into Pam's face. There is a rain of chocolate cake. It is literally raining cake like it rains sparks at the end of "The Natural". Cake and frosting are flying into my IBM Selectric typewriter, my facsimile machine, my telephone answering machine, my teletype, the keyboard of my new PC and my rolodex. Now I am Tippi Hedren in the phone booth scene from "The Birds", taking snapshots with my eyes. Within those split seconds I can only think of the tortures I will inflict upon Charline for the weeks it will take to clean chocolate cake from every pristine mechanism in my cubicle. My sadistic thoughts are interrupted by a shriek from third floor party-crasher, Suzanne: *"Get the knife!"* she blood-curdles.

3:05.7: I wheel around to see Charline holding the "Psycho" knife above her head and looking downward toward the floor. It is now, absolutely, a full-on Brian de Palma movie. The world congeals even more slowly to, say, three frames per second. I take what feels like 20 minutes to turn my head, in askance for help from higher ranks. I spot Leslie and Linda standing like 2 pillars on the periphery. With fabric swatches draped over one shoulder, pearls and corporate ruffles, the two stand erect and immobilized. Clutching plastic champagne flutes, they both maintain a sardonic grin. They have lost it. They have gone into sensory overload and this is not the time to be calling on USC sorority sisters for help. Literally frozen in terror, they have contributed what they could by delivering the cake, and they are maxed out.

3:06: In the most frustrating, agonizing slow motion, I raise myself from my chair. I tilt my head downward to find Pam crawling like a wounded mammal on all fours. *"My eyes!"* she screams. 'Dear God', I think, 'Charline has cut out her eyeballs'. Not so. It seems in the cake smear, Pam has lost her contact lenses and cannot see past her nose. Does that stop Charline? No.

3:06.5: As Charline raises the knife above her head, her eyes fixated on the limping gazelle beneath her, I lunge over my teetery half-wall shelving and tackle Charline, only to have her large but agile body slip from underneath me. Pam claws the ground toward the elevators, reaching out desperately for some landmark, to tell her where she is. I am blinded by flying cake and deafened by shrill screams from the audience. Finally, several of us have piled on top of Charline and peel her fingers from the knife handle. Overhead Brian de Palma shot: a mass of exhausted bodies, slathered in icing and the glint of a steely knife blade reflecting up as we all breathe, heavily.

3:07: Pam, assisted by co-workers has made it to a nearby sofa, awash in frosting with burned out candles, poking out of her mullet. Leslie and Linda remain standing, staring straight ahead, fried. The room is quiet except for more heavy breathing and whimpering sobs from the crowd.

It seems Pam and Charline had had a disagreement.

Leslie and Linda were finally able to move, as they sweetly and gingerly began picking bits of cake from my hair. We were all sent home to await calls from Viacom corporate. It was a big day for us at the 'mount.

Charline was let go.

The "Cheers" TV show heyday happened when I was tied up with school work and I would discover it in re-runs. The show was still in production when I started at Paramount, and all we knew there was some sort of magic happening over on the TV side of the lot—those stages numbered in the 20s.

At Paramount, names like Burrows, Danson, Grammer, Long, Casey, Angell, Lee, Perlman flew across my desk on paperwork, raising question marks for those of us on the movie side, but not until "Cheers" ended, did I start to discover the fun.

I was called in to work for 6 weeks for David Lee, Peter Casey and David Angell, all "Cheers" writers, developing their new show "Wings".

Naturally, Paramount had high hopes. Television Production doyenne Ruth Carpenter had sought me out to make the boys comfortable, and on the first day, I was late for work. I had been given the wrong location for their new offices! Just across from Stage 18 where Bill Holden and Erich von Stroheim had worked, the boys had assembled, and Ruth was waiting for me in the outer office.

I stumbled in at 9:15, frazzled. Ruth began: "At Paramount Pictures, when we pass you the ball, you are expected to run with it!" As if she could tell me anything I didn't already know about Paramount. I dropped my belongings on my desk. I spun myself around and leaned on my desk behind me. "Great!" I yelled sarcastically, "but first someone has to *pass me the ball!*" Ruth left in a huff, but we were very cordial after that. We understood one another.

If you are sure of yourself enough to yell back, and what you're yelling is respectable, it is a sure-fire rite of passage for studio life.

I turned to the inner office door and my 3 bosses popped their heads out, one on top of the other from the inside of the doorframe-- an old

Marx Brothers bit-- frightened by my exchange with Ruth! They had me rolling for 6 weeks. "You really gave it to Ruth!" they chimed.

David, Peter and David built a character for "Wings" based on a tough but harmless, red lip-sticked security guard in charge of our building. We eventually moved to the Wilder Bldg., named for Billy Wilder. Our location across from Stage 18 and my position were both temporary. Perhaps my demise was due to my answering their phone: "We're wilder in Wilder!" I am sorry. I thought it was funny.

My temp career lasted a few months, while I was an actor, and in that time I managed a one week stint working for the great Ted Danson— super tall and super nice. David/Peter/David and Ted were birds of a feather. It was slowly coming together for me. They had the same sense of humor. They were all more clever than me, and I began to appreciate them, even more so, as a group.

Once I inadvertently followed Rhea Perlman from the Gower walk-in to the Admin. Bldg. It became uncomfortable the way it does when both parties realize they are walking the same path. When she turned around to confront me, I said "Yes! I am stalking you!" She screamed with laughter which made me love her all the more. I was so happy she laughed instead of calling Security!

Back to Paramount I went, in 1993, full time, and discovered the "Frasier" set. As a Paramount employee, one kills the afternoon by wandering stage to stage, walking off that 2-martini lunch at Nickodell, to see what my friend Parker, a Wardrobe Coordinator, was up to on Stage 25. I crossed paths with David Hyde Pierce most mornings, coming onto the lot from the Gower gate, shouting a cheerful hello as I circled him on my rollerblades, my mode of transportation from my home at Sunset and La Brea.

I made it my business to find out why he and Parker both worked on Stage 25.

25 was now home to "Frasier", yet another Angell/Casey/Lee production! I trotted onto the stage one lunch hour, and the "Cheers"

bar had been replaced with a Seattle skyline backing, and a split-level condo featuring a creepy Lay-Z-Boy recliner in natty brown, lime green and silver Duck Tape.

I tippy-toed my way upstairs to the Wardrobe area to find Parker, busily prepping for a final dress rehearsal. We screamed and hugged and he said "If you see Kelsey, do not bug him, Rob. I know how you are." "Please, Parker," I rallied. "I am a professional."

I lounged in Marty Craine's recliner, tee-heed with the crew and scurried down the hallways looking for Kelsey to see if I could ruffle his feathers. I had seen Kelsey perform Richard II at the Mark Taper Forum. His was a brilliant portrayal of a rarely performed Shakespearean character.

Parker hustled by me with a flurry of neckties over one shoulder. "Kelsey likes options," he explained. "At least three". "I'll help him pick!" I offered. Parker: "No, you will not." Parker darted into Kelsey's dressing room to lay out said neck ties. Kelsey approached from around the corner with a steely demeanor and a slow, no-nonsense gate. "Hey, Kelsey!" I said goofily, pretending to break the ice like we were old friends. "Hi", he managed back, turning into his dressing room.

John Mahoney was particularly fun, on and off camera, as was David Hyde Pierce, as was Dan Butler who played Bulldog. I was mystified that Kelsey was not funny and affable on the set, to studio drones like me. Then it occurred to me: Dana Gould (The Simpsons) and Kathy Griffin (My Life on the D-List) are just funny people all the time. Kelsey Grammer, maybe not, necessarily. Over the years of spying on the set, I found Kelsey to be more of a studied technician, like Lucille Ball who wasn't a cut-up off camera, but oh so funny on stage where it counted. Plus, Kelsey didn't even know me!

Kelsey carried the weight of a hit show on his shoulders, thereby supporting hundreds or thousands of jobs. No wonder he was serious. I learned by haunting that stage, comedy is a serious business.

Top: *Shooting "Saved By the Bell" with buddy Dave Mecham. Santa Monica, 1991*
Bottom: *Mario Lopez and me on the "Saved By the Bell" set at*
NBC Burbank, singing a duet backstage, ca, 1990

NBC 1989-1993
"Saved By the Bell" Lunch Hour

One of the biggest misconceptions about acting in movies or television is that actors are pampered, setting their own schedule, holed up in their dressing room until they're good n' ready to come to the set. Another myth is that actors get to do as many takes as they want until they get it right. Those two ideas could not be further from the truth.

Yes, yes, yes, if DeNiro wants another go-'round, Marty's not gonna say no, and if Marilyn was late to the set, Cukor would have to make do, but those are rare exceptions. With a union crew of a hundred people, high-priced talent and labor costs, every minute must be accounted for and going into extra days, or minutes, is taboo.

I was an actor in the late 80s and early 90s and like everything in show biz, it seems, I learned it the hard way, including my lesson in 'Punctuality 101'.

I worked on several TV projects for NBC who produced their shows at various locations such as Raleigh Studios, Sunset Gower Studios, as well as the NBC lot in Burbank.

I was doing stand-in work in 1991. Television is perhaps less forgiving than movies, for actors, with its rigid schedule. Production companies are made to produce a finished product once a week like clockwork—and it had better be perfect. There is no such thing as not finishing an episode, and so, there is no such thing as actors flubbing lines or being late or not showing up. From the table read to the taping to post production, it must be a well-oiled machine that cannot be interrupted.

TV stand-ins are hired to play the part of an actor who is unavailable for rehearsals, as opposed to movie stand-ins who are hired for lighting purposes. TV stand-ins are actors and movie stand-ins are bodies picked for their coloring and dimensions, to match a certain actor. Always at the ready, TV stand-ins are expected to know their actor's blocking, and jump into the scene at a moment's notice.

My happiest times as a stand-in all went down on NBC's "Saved By the Bell". I appeared on the show four times, recorded ten voice-overs, and worked as a stand-in for Mark-Paul Gosselaar, Mario Lopez, Dustin Diamond and Dennis Haskins more times than I can count. I wish I could explain the hilarity and hijinx that had me rolling from 1990 to 1992. Like any fun time, it has everything to do with where you are in your own life and the chemistry created by your interaction with those around you. Who knew our little Production Assistant Bethenny Frankel would become a famous zillionaire, or that guest star Leah Remini would earn an Emmy and use that power to fight the evil that is Scientology? From the producers, to the crew to the cast to the extras, that included Casper Van Dien, Denise Richards and Scotty Wolf, "Saved By the Bell" was a joy and non-stop fun. The fact that it became a hit show was icing on the cake.

We weren't supposed to cuss around the "kids" and that, for some nervous reason, made me laugh. As a 27 year-old, I found myself squeezing between flats outside the stage to sneak a ciggie, only to be busted more than once by the always curious and ubiquitous Dustin Diamond. *That* made me laugh. I promised to sneak Dustin beers at the next wrap party if he wouldn't tattle, and *that* made me laugh. The effortless and breezy attitudes of producers Peter Engle and Franco Bario, undercut by their steely resolve, when pushed, made me laugh. My counterpart, our female stand-in, had the God-given name of Penny Nickels. It, and she, made me scream with laughter every day. Production team members Ellie, Maria and Casey were all three, warm blankets of love, for real, so their occasional scathing zingers would make me howl all the more. I admired our director, Don Barnhart because every week he did what I could never do. He made the whole thing work, despite our antics. He might spend five minutes listening carefully to the crazy suggestion of a guest star, stroll to his podium, grab his family-size barrel of Tums and glug down tens of tablets (which made me laugh). Not a fun moment for him, but an hilarious visual. And every zany week, I got to play a teenager. It was wonderful.

One glorious day I was standing in for the star, Mark-Paul Gosselaar. We were shooting the NBC show, that day at Sunset Gower Studios, the old Columbia Pictures lot. I looked nothing like Mark-Paul, but given a backwards baseball cap and a letterman's jacket, I could duplicate his energy if necessary. M-P had no scheduled time away that day. He was in good health, good spirits, and we giggled the morning away as I shadowed his blocking, marking my script as I was paid to do, however casually. Lark Voorhies had coined his new nickname, "Bottle Blonde" and we giggled about it incessantly. It was one of those days where I felt like Ethel Merman's understudy for "Gypsy". M-P was super solid and I would absolutely not be called upon to assay his role.

Lunch was from 12 to 1 and I sauntered over to Denny's restaurant across the street with the super-pretty Tiffany-Amber Thiessen, the aforementioned Penny Nickels and a couple other kids. We grabbed the check at 12:45 and upon exiting Denny's I told the gang I would be right along but I had to use the pay phone. "It's 5 till," warned Penny Nickels. "Don't worryyy," I said. "I'll be right there! Plus, M-P is here—I won't even be used today." "Whatever you say...", Penny Nickels trailed.

I sprawled out my paperwork before me in the phone booth that used to stand proudly at Sunset and Gower, with its gleaming interior counter and plastic-bound phone book on a snake chain. I finished side-stepping my bill over the phone with the Gas Company and glanced at my chunky watch, which read 1:02.

OK, here's where it gets weird and difficult to equate to the normal world. Ya know how when your dad says to be home by midnight and you notice it's 3am and you're still at Flippers Roller Disco? I became a sweaty fish-eye lens subject, just like Roy Scheider in "Jaws" when he sees Alex Kintner being eaten by the shark.

My world became molasses. I left my paperwork in the pristine phone booth and clawed my way across Gower Street despite honking horns and near-fatal collisions. I was in the stretching hallway from "Poltergeist". It was bad.

The stage building layouts at Sunset Gower are not kidding around. They are old and rickety with a maze of inner corridors that finally vomit you onto the stage itself. My panic was not unfounded. When a director calls "back at 1 pm", he is more than serious. As I thundered through the hallways, which sounded like I was stampeding down the hallway of a mobile home, I heard a strangely similar sound in the distance. Yes—someone like me was late too, coming from the opposite direction. Please, God in Heaven, it couldn't be Mark-Paul. I pounded toward the stage door, as did the criminal coming toward me. The disembodied footsteps now had a name—a hyphenated name, and that hyphenated name was Mark-Paul. We came nose to nose, out of breath and faces blanched. We looked into each other's eyes and hiss-whispered, simultaneously: "Oh, shit!" We were goners and we knew it because it was now 1:05. We opened the insulated door together.

There was Don, our director, script in hand on the set, playing M-P's part. Ironically, it was a whimsical setting. A proscenium stage within a stage, where the fanciful gaggle of Bayside High stars would perform their charming version of "Snow White". Don was reading a scene as Zack, with Dustin Diamond. Ever so slowly the entire cast and crew craned around to look at us with disgust. Their necks creaked with disgust. Their searchlight eyes flashed up and down with disgust. Dustin bore a Cheshire grin that taunted us with disgust (and merriment). Casey and Ellie and Maria could not look at us, and they turned away with disgust, embarrassed to have ever made our acquaintance.

M-P and I crept toward the light. "Hey—hey you guys-- what—what's goin' on?", we managed with fake nonchalance. Don rose, slowly, letting his script drop to the floor with a ruffle and a thud, and walked toward us with purposeful determination while everyone hung their heads, as they might, before a public execution. I'm pretty sure some made the sign of the cross. We felt the nooses tighten with every step of Don's approach. An ethical legacy of punctuality and promptness had built that old Columbia Pictures stage. Clark Gable in "It Happened One Night", Barbara Stanwyck in "Golden Boy", and the Columbia pantheon of players from any given era floated above Don like taunting, ghostly school children, infusing him with self-righteous energy and wagging their fingers at us, ceremoniously. Don stopped ten feet from us. His voice was quiet but intense and his eyes burned over the top of his scary half-glasses. He began a 2-minute growl: something about unprofessional and replaceable and pathetic and sad. Poor M-P had to walk into the scene as his not-a-care-in-the-world character, while I slunk into the shadows.

I trembled like a wet dog until Penny Nickels, in an unrelated moment of desperation and surrender, handed me the LA Times crossword and asked If I possibly knew the answer for 17-down. Franco had witnessed my dressing down. He glanced at me and shook his thick mane of hair, trying to hide his crack of a smile. M-P finished blocking the scene and we couldn't look at each other without eliciting nervous blurts of laughter. And ever so slowly, we were back.

One of my many headshots I used as an actor in the early 90s.

The Names Project AIDS Memorial Quilt was an exhibition housed in Washington, D.C. At one time, it covered the entire Mall between Capitol Hill and the Washington Monument. Large sections of the quilt were dedicated to those who had died of the then unmanageable disease. The sections were stitched together; each one emblazoned with the name of the departed and decorated by loved ones, as an expression of warmth and grief, to mourn the dead.

The Quilt traveled to Los Angeles and was exhibited at our Pacific Design Center. Wooch and I felt we should go see it, to pay homage to so many friends and colleagues who had passed. On our way in, Wooch asked me if I was happy with my commercial agent. I sighed and admitted he hadn't sent me on any auditions in months! "They're all alike," we decided, "only interested in the flavor of the week."

We turned the corner into the huge hall, lined with hanging Quilt sections and there before me was the name of my agent, Perry Hawthorne. He had died and I almost dropped to my knees. I started to cry with embarrassment at how I had put my shoddy little acting career first, before wondering if Perry was OK. What a lesson in compassion and ego. It still haunts me.

Always on the lookout for a new agent, I found an agency, supposedly in Pasadena, soliciting new talent. They agreed to see me so off I went, traversing the ancient Arroyo Seco Parkway (America's first freeway) until I came to Exit 51. This was not Pasadena but rather an off-ramp in the woods, somewhere beyond downtown near Chavez Ravine. It was a remote location to say the least.

My 1978 Chevette hatchback crunched its way over the graveled parking area. It was an uncharacteristically dark and gloomy day in "Los Angeles/Pasadena-ish", but luckily the address I was given had a neon dragon attached to the building, buzzing on and off, to illuminate the way. Yes, as my tires sunk into the rocky parking area

I became painfully aware that the "agency" for which I would be reading, occupied the second floor above a Chinese restaurant.

I crept into the interior back entrance and looked up the wooden stair passage. There were 3 obstacles blocking my path: a 20-pound bag of fortune cookies and 2 beautiful but condescending Chinese girls with thick, blunt bangs, tight silk mini-dresses with turned up collars, and smoking filtered cigarillos, on the stairs. I wish I was making this up. I thought I was "Thoroughly Modern Millie", destined for white slavery for sure.

I stepped over the giant bag of cookies and one girl gave me a head bump toward the door upstairs. We spoke the international language of show biz as I was a dopey white boy carrying an 8x10 head shot. Upstairs was an agent sitting at a desk in a large room with a hardwood floor. He wanted a cold reading, to which I was accustomed, and naturally he had chosen a monologue from some Viet Nam play. Viet Nam plays were all the rage at the time for those of us 20-something males. I had coerced my day off work from NBC which was no small feat, wound up in the forest just beyond the Los Angeles Zoo, had been dissed by cigarillo smokers with a battitude, blinded by a buzzing neon dragon before me, and now handed yet another Viet Nam scenario to be performed cold, regarding being blown to bits with an arm missing and my best friend dead. I was so angry I started to cry before I began the monologue. "Good," said the agent, "gooood…"

My Larry Edmunds script was wet and there were several bodily fluids on the floor of the agency when I finished. The agent looked terrified as I handed him back his script. I think he thought I was "disturbed". He didn't sign me but eventually sent me out on some calls which I did not book. It was a weird f

In today's lexicon, "Michael Jackson" is really one word, for obvious reasons. Have you noticed no one ever says just "Michael", when speaking about him? He's never called "Mike" or "Mr. Jackson if you're nasty". He will always be one word: "Michaeljackson". It's odd, but comfortable.

After fleeing NBC one day, I found a message on my answering machine from dear pal and Hollywood gad-about Paul Kawasaki. Paul had his hands in *everything* from music to movies to publishing. "We're seeing Michaeljackson tonight," Paul informed. It's a weird set up—just go with it…" So as always with Kawasaki, I let the good times roll.

The weird set-up was as follows: in preparation for the 1991 MTV Music Awards, Michaeljackson was slated to perform two songs: "Black or White" and "Man in the Mirror". The awards were a few months away, but given Michaeljackson's grueling schedule, there was no time to perform at the live telecast. An airplane hangar at Santa Monica Airport had been rented and a replica of the Awards stage in NYC was built there, at which Michaeljackson would perform now, to be broadcast later. Fifty or so Hollywood insiders—me and Paul, chief among them—were recruited to stand along the periphery of the stage and fist pump in the vacuous hangar while Michaeljackson and Slash, sang and played their hearts out. It would be inserted into the televised show later. And lemme tellya, those two crazy rock n' roll icons gave till it hurt, just the same for 50 as 5,000. Pros.

Paul and I crunched into the Santa Monica hangar parking lot, just a stumbly clunk from Sepulveda Blvd. What might have been a tedious night, turned into a magical list of who's who, important only to me, perhaps, but still, a night I never wanted to end.

"Angel!", yelled David Mecham as he emerged from the hangar to greet us. Lifelong pal and super Hollywood pundit, Dave Mecham will always embody show business. "Look who's here!" gushed Mecham, pointing to Jim Sweeney. Jim happens to be the brother of Saturday Night Live's mega-talent, Julia Sweeney. Jim is adorable but what made it special is that his all-time crush Tammy was also in the house. It is a mystical chain of events that bring show biz entities together and tonight was no exception. By God, those two hooked up there, got married, and Jim n' Tammy Sweeney have been together ever since!

As sparks were flying between Jim and Tammy to burn down the airport, who should I spy, but Brooke Shields, holding Bubbles, Michaeljackson's adorable primate! Inside the hangar, it was a surreal world like stepping into Willie Wonka's factory. Not only was the stage set for glamour, but there was Brooke, and—who's this? Brooke's incorrigible mother Terri. Mrs. Shields thrust forward her arm, blocking me from greeting Brooke. "Hold it," Terri growled, "you're not laying a hand on my daughter!" "It's true, I love your daughter," I said, quickly and defensively, "but I'm after the monkey!" We screamed and laughed and screamed and laughed. Brooke, who was tending not only to Bubbles, but to several of Michaeljackson's primates, handed me the famous chimp, warmly.

Michaeljackson was super-gracious, as was Slash, coming into our fake mosh pit several times to express their gratitude, although the pleasure was all ours for every one of the eight takes required.

Then Dan the Man appeared! Dan the Man was a beautiful dancer I had met at Paramount where we both worked. He was wearing metallic body paint and giant wings on his arms, which he showcased behind Michaeljackson during "Man in the Mirror". As Dan the Man took flight behind Michaeljackson, Jim and Tammy made out in the corner. The rest of us shrieked at the apron of the stage while Terri and Brooke managed the monkeys. It was a bizarre, brilliant night that could only happen in Hollywood, U.S.A. (or the Santa Monica Airport).

Scouting locations for the Dolgen shoot, ca. 1995.

Paramount Pictures 1993-1997
Harrison Ford and Dean Jones

My time at Paramount was divided in two when I escaped for four years to be an actor, or, mostly a stand-in for actors. I stood-in for the purposeful and kind "Brady Bunch" patriarch, Robert Reed, and also for perennial Disney favorite, Dean Jones, not to mention the "Saved By the Bell" boys.

Like Robert Reed, and really, anyone at his level, Dean Jones was a consummate professional. We were working on a TV movie in Laguna Beach, and one morning around 7 am, while standing on the periphery of the grey and misty outdoor set-up, Dean turned to me. "Could I *please* get a *chair*?!". He barked his request to no one in particular. "Is it *weird* that I remember when actors got *chairs*?!" His blunt and plaintive desperation was my first laugh of the morning, although Dean was serious as a heart attack. I said, "I'm not really the 'chair guy', Dean, but let me see what I can do". Finally I produced a sturdy director's chair for him. Hell, I was happy to do it. He starred in "Million Dollar Duck" and could do no wrong in my book.

Let's face it; I was in awe of Dean. Whether he liked it or not, he was my youth. There are no words to describe the wonder of warming up to Dean at age 5 wearing footy pajamas, sandwiched between my parents and sister at the drive-in, and then, 25 years later, working with Dean, the 3-dimensional person. Over the drive-in speaker, his voice was commanding but tinny, and now it was wrapping around me, coming at me directly, fueled by a chair shortage! I couldn't get over it and he must have wondered why I had an ear-to-ear grin. If he had asked for the Hope Diamond, I would have rustled it up in 10 minutes. I was impressionable, to say the least. I had, after all witnessed the magical configuration of Dean with Hayley Mills, Suzanne Pleshette, Sandy Duncan, a cat, a duck—and now me!

The real thrill of working with Dean hinged on my infatuation with his portrayal of Robert in Stephen Sondheim's "Company". It's the role of a lifetime in a seminole American musical, and for as much time as we spent kibitzing between takes and crossword-puzzling the day away, I could not bring myself to ask him about it. When I finally got up the nerve, he answered, "It was so painful!" I asked why. Dean explained that he was going through his own arduous divorce at the time, which mirrored his character's loneliness in "Company". Robert cannot find anyone special to share his life with, however surrounded by coupled friends, urging him to do so. The company of "Company" was running its pre-Broadway run in Boston and Dean found himself in nightly conversations with his children before going on to play the buoyant but tortured Robert, echoing his own life. I got my answer, having always wondered what was behind his recording of the show-stopping ballad, "Being Alive." It is a taught rendition and high-strung with desperation and pathos. So that was it. He had drawn it directly from his life at the time.

When my acting career began to hemorrhage, I crawled back to Paramount and begged for employment. Eventually I became a photo editor in their Creative Advertising Dept. I created photo shoots, just wrangled others, and for some I merely whisked in and out with contracts for others to sign and artist's sketches of the expected visual set-ups.

The Tom Clancy-authored trilogy, beginning with "The Hunt For Red October" and "Patriot Games", starring Alec Baldwin and Harrison Ford as Jack Ryan, was in production for its third installment, "Clear and Present Danger". A quick portrait shoot of Harrison Ford had been arranged on the shooting stage that day, where a plain seamless backing was hung, off in a corner. We were granted access to Harrison for only 15 minutes so timing was critical and execs were on edge. I received a call at the Photo Empire, my sprawling amalgam of light-boxed counters and cabinets containing film and digital records. Our wunderkind Creative Director Bryan Allen was calling from Stage 31, along with vibrant Paramount executive, Lucia Ludovico. They had forgotten the concept sketches and asked me to bring them.

Bryan understood me, as a person, and had a thorough knowledge of what my demeanor may be in this situation. "When you bring the sketches in", he warned, "do not make a big fuss, do not lollygag, do not comment on Harrison's cute fedora or his physical stature, or Lucia's new haircut", he pleaded. "Just bring the sketches in an envelope, hand them to me and go." "Bryan, *honestly!*" I chided, trying to communicate that I could handle this without incident. "Bryan, I am a professional—not sure if you're aware of that-- and I can totally do this." "Good," he trumped.

I shimmied down the narrow breezeway between soundstages, sketches in hand. I threw wide the enormous door to Stage 31, as there was no red light turning, and sashayed in. I could see Bryan and Harrison and Lucia, and photographer Lee Varis encamped in the far corner of the cavernous stage. I strode toward them, purposefully.

But wait, between me and them was the freestanding set in the middle of the stage, of a big beautiful room. Through the plexi-glass windows and 2x4 wall supports I saw rich draperies and crown molding and— what's this? Presidential seals! Taken with the spectacular set, I forgot my mission. I approached the beautiful room and entered. I was in the White House Oval Office. I sunk to my ankles in the plush carpeting and turned 360 degrees to take it all in. I was in Washington DC and feeling a bit intimidated, fearful Donald Rumsfeld may enter and have me killed. No matter what my mission, no matter what decorum may be expected, I am a sucker for sets and I cannot help it. Muuust exploooore. The Oval Office stood between me and my goal, and I chose the former, skipping down Pennsylvania Avenue, unfettered by National Security or Secret Service.

In the same way that I would not go to my car at night, through the dark streets of the outdoor Brooklyn backlot sets, for fear of mugging, I was completely taken in by being in the President's Office. I could smell the roses as I turned, looking out to what should have been the Rose Garden. But wait-- there was Bryan, planted firmly, motioning to me with his hand. Oops.

Everyone was waiting. Harrison, who was wearing a khaki trench coat, also wore a dower look on his face—maybe in character or maybe not. I walked toward the photo shoot set-up. Then a full, rich voice boomed from off-stage: "Rob? Rob, is that *you*?!" It was one of two people. It could only be the voice of God or Dean Jones! Dean burst from the shadows, face orange with make-up and wearing something very formal. "What are you *doing* here?!", I screeched. "I'm in this crazy thing," he said, like it was nothing. "I can't beleeeeve it!", I squealed. We went on for some time as Harrison and my superiors looked on, perplexed and showing early signs of livid.

I broke away with some lingered shoulder patting and groveled toward the waiting party, affecting a subservient apology with my body language. I exited the same way, as if setting a movie projector on Reverse.

I am *sorry*, but sometimes when you run into the Oval Office and a former colleague, with whom you are obsessed, rules are broken. I never heard about it from Bryan. I think they may have been stumped by my giddiness or maybe they got it. Maybe Harrison had seen "The Love Bug" and therefore understood the "Clear and Present Danger" shoot was in league with my having reconnected briefly, with the marvelous Dean Jones.

Sherry Lansing

I love Sherry Lansing, and no one loves her more than me—not her husband Bill Friedkin, not the populace of the American Midwest, from where she hails—no one. One minute she was producing "Fatal Attraction" for Paramount and the next minute she was running the studio. Her presence was felt as the embodiment of show business savvy and the barometer of success. She is simply, Sherry, and that is, precisely, all you need to know.

One autumn evening in 1996, gal-pal Claudette and I decided to take a walk down Paramount's Marathon Paseo (we like to keep things Spanish in Southern California), a long stretch of brick footing that ran from the Marathon Bldg. where we worked, to the Company Store. The Paseo is about a football field long and at its end you'll find a pot of gold (a Bank of America ATM).

Claudette and I had to work late that night, and so at 6pm we decided to breeze the Paseo, get some cash, and return to hunker down and pray for daylight. It was a balmy October evening and during our stroll back we found ourselves gliding by the very spot where employees gather each December to light the Tree. A bit misty-eyed and full of sentiment, Claudette and I began regaling each other with our fondest memories of the Tree Lighting, from seasons past.

The Paramount Tree Lighting is a special and wondrous event. I have called in a multitude of drive-on passes, way past my allotted amount, so friends could witness the spectacle. Nestled in the crux of the lot, in our Commons if you will, the tree typically stands 20 feet high, and on the designated day, it is flanked by a choir robed in red and white, endless tables of food, a small orchestra and more good will than can be imagined. It is the one afternoon, on that brisk December day, when everyone is completely nice to each other. We bury the hatchet for a couple hours to say Happy Holidays, Happy Hanukah, Merry Christmas, Have a Great December, et al.

The zenith of that event comes with Sherry Lansing taking the podium. A hush would fall over all the Whos in Paramount Who-ville and we listened with awe and respect. We didn't get to see our Sherry very often so it was quite a treat.

"This is my favorite time of year," she would begin, "and the production slate for the coming year looks better than ever!" We would scream and cry and applaud, so happy to be part of magic in the making. Then Sherry, with great pride, would bring up the oldest living male and female employees to have them push the fake button to light the tree. After a brief introduction, Stan and Barb, let's call them, would hit the fake button—a huge, glowing, half-sphere of plexi, courtesy the Property Dept. A union electrician would be only half-hidden to some employees, and could be seen, jamming a plug into a socket. We would all purr "Ooohhhh" as the massive tree raced to the heavens in electrical light. Cue the chorus and let the merriment begin! Grips and executives would engage in handshakes and back-slapping—truly a moment to witness for anyone who doubts the power of the holidays and good will toward men.

So there we were, Claudette and I on this October evening, reminiscing and anticipatory of the coming winter celebration. The lot was empty now, with only the clickety-clack of a man and woman a few yards behind us.

As we passed the sacred Tree spot, I launched into it: "Who am I?! Who am I?!". Then, doing my best Sherry Lansing impersonation: "This is my favorite time of year". "Stop!" cried Claudette. The two of us staggered down the Paseo like two drunken sailors. Then I yelled, "Girl-- the day they call *us* to light the Tree is the day we *walk*—am I *right*?" "You are *soooo right*," Claudette agreed. Claudette and I were weeping now, doubled over in a sort of hysteria, re-enacting Paramount's annual blessed event. We went insane for a moment, over our own comedic genius.

The couple behind us grew quiet, silently observing. Claudette and I collected ourselves so as not to faint. The couple passed by, looking at us queerly, almost painfully. "Oh, well," we thought. It was only some stodgy man and… Sherry Lansing. Oops. Our tears turned from mirth to fear. We crawled to a nearby bench, wheezing, in an effort to plan some sort of exit strategy for leaving Paramount. Firing us would clearly be the first order of business for Sherry the next day.

We had seen her make steely eye contact with us both, but who would be first, tomorrow? We made a pact. When Judith (Sherry's assistant) calls and asks one of us for our "Social", we would tell the other immediately, and then just run. We knew we were goners and it was only a matter of when and how. Claudette wore giant sunglasses to work the following morning, and a hat. I went with the penitentiary look: black trousers and a simple white shirt—face scrubbed and ready for execution. We were both "Dead Man Walking".

Do you know, the call never came? To this day, I can see Sherry's black mane, whipping around, shooting daggers with her eyes. She knew. We knew. But she never bothered with us. And that's our Sherry. I had a few casual conversations with Sherry after that. I congratulated her on adding her own recipe of chilled cucumber soup to the Commissary menu. She called on me to make photographs of an event she couldn't attend. Whether she remembered that October evening or not—whether she cared or not, she is a bigger person than me, and that's why I love my Sherry Lansing. She is mine and no one else's.

Jon Dolgen was a distant fellow to those of us in the Paramount trenches. He was, after all, the leader of Viacom Entertainment and Paramount was just one of Viacom's many holdings. Mr. Dolgen had called upon the Paramount Advertising Dept. to set up a cursory photo shoot so he might have new headshots to supply the endless need for trade paper stories swirling around him at their center.

Beloved executive mainstay Nancy Goliger, and prolific art director Tracy Weston, and myself, by proxy, were tasked with the shoot. The three of us trotted around the lot one balmy afternoon, location scouting if you will, for vistas in which to feature Mr. Dolgen. We approached it with an Annie Liebovitz sensibility, storyboarding ideas of Jon looking sternly to the Paramount gates while bathing in the Marathon Fountain, or nestled in the shadows of the Property Dept., looking wryly toward Stage 18. While scampering about the back lot, Nancy made a pit stop to go over some advertising ideas with director Peter Weir for his picture "The Truman Show". "Peter", Nancy called, as the three of us shimmied through a shanty town of Star Waggon trailers. Exhausted from a day's shooting on the film, Peter emerged and invited us aboard. I had been in awe of Peter since "Gallipoli" and became somewhat lightheaded in his presence. All I recall is that he was quiet and kind and we three were back to location scouting.

We pushed concepts that would suggest Dolgen owned this town and ruled it with an iron fist. The fact that it was true, rendered the concepts less clever and much less charming. Dolgen opted for a simple coat and tie look, at his conference table. Our creativity was squelched one minute and elevated the next when we found out Dolgen had requested his college pal, Tom Bianchi to shoot him. Tom had surrounded himself with beautiful, fit men in recent years, and had published several coffee table books featuring those men at his pool and around his home in various stages of undress. Tracy, Nancy and I were delighted with Dolgen's choice, fingers crossed for a fun, creative experience after all.

Tom arrived the day of the shoot with his handsome assistant and we were off and running to meet the chief. We were met by Publicity icon Allison Jackson and all four of Mr. Dolgen's secretaries. Ten of us now, bombarded Jon's office, scooting him toward his conference room. He giggled along quietly, flashing his razor-sharp blue eyes, and sharing anecdotes about his daughters and his reluctance to being photographed.

Tracy and I flew around Jon in circles, teasing his hair and tugging at his shirt and slacks to remove any wrinkles. We pinched his cheeks for color, told bawdy jokes to get some big smiles, and mentioned many times that he "didn't seem like a big corporate meany at *all!*" "Jon," I gushed, "the trades are *liars!* You're the sweetest man, ever!" Jon pretended to blush and everyone screamed uproariously. We pinched, we pulled, we did another set up, we laughed, we cried and even draped ourselves across our new buddy for a couple private shots.

The shoot was a success. Relaxed and cheerful, Nancy and I hung with Dolgen's assistants, titter-tattering about when they could expect proofs, interspersed with peels of "Wasn't that *fun?*", etc., etc.

From the corner of my eye I could see that Jon had gone into his annexed conference room for a meeting with several black-suited Japanese businessmen. There was lots of bobbing and half-bows happening but no one was sitting.

Amid the sighs of confidence and revelry that Nancy and I were enjoying with the Dolgen team, the rumblings of a small earthquake could be felt nearby—or was it the pounding approach of an angry man? As I turned to my right I saw what appeared to be a 7-foot fire hydrant, thick and forged of iron, bent slightly at its center, lurching forward into our little after party. It was Jon, but a very different Jon. One member of his meeting, apparently a critical component, had not arrived.

Mr. Dolgen approached his support staff and planted himself like the final stone atop the tallest Pyramid of Giza. His face was damp and red and he began to yell. He was able to unhinge his jaw slightly like an anaconda, and a thunderous roar of expletives came from his body. His piercing blue eyes that the camera had loved were now blood-shot knives, hunting and darting for an answer. Spittle flew from his mouth and his red face seemed to be a conduit for underworld demons who might emerge to take over all that is holy. It was the chore of his assistance team to ensure the meeting went without a hitch and now a puzzle piece was missing. One of the quaking four bravely stepped a quarter step forward to explain the puzzle piece was en route.

In animal-like desperation to be anywhere but here, Nancy and I struggled to remove our bodies from the mayhem, fighting the absurdity of our own sluggish motor skills. We turned, grabbing at carpet and air toward the exit until we had reached the safety of First Floor, Admin. Walking with a purposeful gate, and shaken, we made our way down the Marathon Paseo, back to our home in the Advertising Dept.

"When worlds collide…" I shuddered, philosophically, wishing I had not seen Dolgen's strident side. Nancy nodded.

Jon Dolgen was good to us, after all and who knows what issues surrounded the meeting with the Japanese businessmen? My shock was a reaction to my own behavior, recalling how I had taken liberties, acting overly familiar with someone I had just met, and realizing I had put my hand in a risky cage.

"*Titanic*"

"Titanic" is a James Cameron picture, developed and produced by Twentieth Century Fox around 1996. When production costs crept passed 250 million, Fox's beloved production chief Bill Mechanic was dispatched to Baja, Mexico where the film was being shot, to have a word with Cameron, regarding escalating costs.

Rumors from Baja to Century City, spoke of Bill sliding into James's trailer, and all the screaming and trailer-rocking that ensued. Bill emerged, minus an arm and a leg perhaps (kidding), but with a message to Paramount Pictures, asking for a 60 million dollar investment in exchange for domestic distribution rights. What did Cameron care if the money came from another studio? And Mechanic was happy to share the costs.

At Paramount, we growled and rolled our eyes at the thought of backing some step child disaster film from the Pico Blvd. war horse. Because I was a photo editor at the 'mount, the 30,000 still images began rolling in, so art directors and designers could begin a domestic marketing campaign pitch. Ironically, those stills would follow me to the Fox lot when I switched studios, like a big jackpot of thorns. My many boxes of images I had organized, came back to me like Dickens' Ghost of Christmas Past, when I began to take over the conservation of the same original photographs for Twentieth Century Fox International distribution. I ended up managing what the whole world saw, in stills, that is. It was a thrilling job and a big job.

We had nurtured Leo DiCaprio at Paramount ever since he appeared in "What's Eating Gilbert Grape". And this Kate Winslet chick was supposed to be pretty good. Gloria Stuart was a surprise. I had so admired her in the Universal horror movies of the 1930s, and we all loved Bill Paxton, no matter what. So it was mostly with an optimistic gate that the Paramount Marketing staff, and associates, trapesed into the on-lot Theatre that day to see what Jim Cameron and his Baja crew had cobbled together. "This oughta be rich," I said in Hollywood smug to a Marketing pal.

It was rich in every way. The quality was sublime, and it made millions and millions on opening night, and then billions worldwide when I lost count. In fact, it became the most profitable motion picture we had ever seen.

We sat silently through the film's 15 minutes of end credits, and when the screen ran dark, we peeled ourselves from the cushy seats. Tracy Weston, Greg Kachel (advertising exec diva) and I, found ourselves trudging up a flight of exterior stairs leading to our offices on the second floor of the Marathon Bldg. We felt we had been through a war. We were elated and exhausted. "What the hell *was* that?", asked Tracy. "I'm not sure", I mumbled, motioning hopelessly for a cigarette. "This is gonna be big." said Tracy, taking a long drag. Kachel said, "Gimme a cigarette". I said, "I didn't know you smoked." Kachel said, "I don't".

*Dwarfed by the looming "Seven Year Itch" mural
painted on the side of Stage 10.
Twentieth Century Fox, ca. 2010.*

Twentieth Century Fox 1998-2011
Nigel Arthur

March, 1998: We find a beautiful Marlene Dietrich photo shoot in the Fox Photo Archive, but cannot identify the photographer.

June, 2000: I travel to London on holiday. While perusing bookstores, I purchase a book called *Heads and Tails*, a photograph book, lavishly illustrated by Britain's premiere portrait photographer, Cornel Lucas. The jacket shows a photo of Marlene Dietrich—an image from the shoot we had discovered in our vaults at Fox! At last, I can put the name Cornel Lucas to the image, which until now had been a mystery to us in the states. I haggle with the book seller, as the jacket was torn. I never do that in L.A., but I think haggling feels very European. They give me a 5 pound discount so I pay 15 pounds for the book!

July, 2004: I am going to London on business and have the British Film Institute scheduled as a visit to explore any Fox images housed there. What better gift could I bring but a print of the Dietrich portrait, shot by their beloved British photographer? I arrive at 21 Stephen Street, Dietrich print boxed under one arm and I am greeted by their photograph curator, leaning down the stair at me in the lobby, pulling back his great, thick hair. "I'm Nigel Arthur," he says.

June, 2005: Nigel traverses the Atlantic and comes to work for us in the Photo Archive at Fox for three months at a time—two summers— where we enjoy movie-going at the Hollywood Bowl, the Los Angeles Theatre and Grauman's Chinese, to name a few. Naturally we make time to visit bars on Pico Blvd. and we see Pat Benatar at a roadhouse above Malibu. Nigel, the pasty Brit with the luxurious hairline had come to embody for me, summer fun on the Golden Coast.

December, 2007: I travel to London to give a talk at the BFI in their theatre on London's South Bank. While concluding the Q&A portion at the end of my lecture, I hear a voice out there in the dark say, "Hello, Rob!" "Who is it?" I call back like an amped up Oprah Winfrey. He says, "Cornel!" Well I can hardly believe it. 90 year-old Cornel Lucas has come to my talk—the man whose Dietrich shoot we discovered in our archive at Fox and again at Foiles Book Store in Charing Cross. I introduce Cornel to the crowd and they are thrilled. It is a dream come true, meeting England's great photographer at my oration on movie stills. He has come to see me, but it should have been he on the stage.

From the BFI Theatre I am whisked to a book-signing for the Fox book I had edited, and then to a dinner for the event. I never expect applause from the Brits, but there it was as I entered. For ten seconds, I am the teapot at the talent show once again. Cornel is there, Nigel is there, a new friend Rhidian is there. It is the most glamorous night of my life.

In the months that followed, Nigel became even more intrigued with Cornel Lucas and Nigel contacted Cornel to make a short documentary about his Dietrich photograph sitting, which is entitled "Cornel Lucas A Portrait".

Joan Collins

Joan can be a prickly pear. Since meeting her, however, I have become bored with average, ho-hum pears and want only the prickly ones. She is everything one would expect from Alexis Colby Carrington Dexter Lloyd III x 10 + infinity, or whatever her final character name was on ABC's "Dynasty", but the best part of Joan is what you can't expect.

Razor-sharp, Joan lives the Boy Scout motto: "Be Prepared". I presume she infiltrated the Boy Scouts and merit-badged her way to Eagle Scout in no time, sporting a be-jeweled satin neckerchief.

But Joan, unlike Alexis, shies away from topics like "sex" and "medical procedures". She is human, after all, and furthermore, British. As such, Joan often communicates with non-verbal restraint and conservation of effort. An arched brow and subtle grin are the foundation of JoanSpeak. She gave the twentieth century one of its most indelible characters, and compelling as her character study may be, I found Joan, the person, infinitely more fascinating than any character she played.

Joan and her affable husband, Percy Gibson, came to me in 2009 to acquire photographs from the Fox collection. Percy is handsome and he bridges that gap, when necessary, between rigid good manners and down-home fun. The Christmas card following their wedding in Hawaii, showed the nuptial couple in a very genuine moment that was truly... heartwarming. As a photo editor, I rarely use that adjective. They have something special.

In the 1950s, Joan was contracted to Fox for 7 years. In those days, contract players were shackled by the studio, and during Joan's time at Fox, actresses may as well have been shackled to Daryl Zanuck's office. Zanuck is legendary for his stress-relieving "nooners", involving various starlets. When I asked Joan about it all, she demurred. But she allowed Percy to expound on her behalf, on an uncomfortable moment with Zanuck. From my digging and cajoling over future meetings with the Gibsons, I am certain that Joan was a good girl regarding Daryl's advances. I know, I know-- it's confounding. We presume she might have eventually married him, used him up, wore him out and tossed him to the curb, adding "Zanuck" to her jar of last names. But remember, that's Alexis, not Joan.

I learned something about judging people. It was rude of me to ask in the first place. I later thought to myself that I would never have asked that of someone in another profession. And further, it was silly of me to put upon Joan, presupposed traits, because of sexy roles she may have played. I was embarrassed that I had fallen prey to the scandal sheet and its stereotyping. Sexual predators that she plays, aside, she's still my Eagle Scout in cashmere hiking socks. And that cashmere doesn't earn itself, honey. She's a planner. She may have dated Warren Beatty like much of the 213 Area Code, but Joan pointed out that Warren proposed marriage. She was the only girl to get a ring. I won't say she's beyond reproach. She's above it.

More so than any Fox star I worked with, Joan has honed and perfected the gracious art of business payback. Although helping her was part of my job, I pushed the limits of time and money. Joan and Percy sensed it, showing their appreciation by offering me house seats to Joan's play "Legends", and more than once, whisked me off to super-fun lunches; most notably, a breezy afternoon at the Beverly Hills Hotel Polo Lounge.

For the Polo Lounge, I thought I had nailed Beverly Hills casual chic in white jeans and a rumply, untucked Calvin Klein shirt. As I approached the table, I knew I was wrong. I could only see my lunch partners from the waist up. Joan wore a white fedora-- the kind you get in the fine Bourbon St. shops in New Orleans, a fitted dark grey pin-striped gangster blazer and low cut silk blouse. Percy wore a navy sport coat over a starched shirt printed with a dark violet, big gingham check. They were a spectacular sight. Percy's pocket handkerchief matched his shirt!

They masked their reaction beautifully, saving the day. "Calvin?" Joan chirped. I thought, 'My God. She is better than David Blaine! How does she know my shirt is Calvin Klein?" Like I said, *razor*-sharp.

I like to think my slobby appearance facilitated what turned out to be a wonderful, relaxed and languid lunch. Joan sent her salmon back (prickly) so we shared my fries for a while. Percy was in the midst of writing patter for Joan's upcoming cabaret act in New York so we punched up some lines-- a thrill for me. The soul-healing Marianne Williamson and cute entourage draped by to say hello and I dedicated myself to a steady stream of gin and tonics. For me, it was Heaven.

One spring afternoon, Joan and I sat alone in the Photo Archive at Twentieth Century Fox, pouring over images from her 1957 movie, "The Sea Wife". On that day, Joan was wearing a duo-toned brown suede Chanel suit.

Let me just say it again: suede Chanel.

I was never a big "clothes person", but when Joan wears Chanel to your office, you will, in fact, be into clothes. I'm just saying, it's potentially life-changing.

We were looking at a special shoot from a film in which Joan plays a nun. I was staring at a 4x5 color transparency of her in her nun's habit and said to her, "look how beautiful this shot is." She looked at the image, fondly, and went back to work. "Buuuut..." I continued, "I was raised by a *flock* of nuns, and they could never hope to look as good as you because they were not allowed to wear make-up." Joan turned to me. "Why do you think I would wear make-up if I was playing a nun?" "Joan, Joan, *Joan!*" I pleaded, "there is no such thing as going before the cameras without a little somethin' on your face-- little rouge, little foundation, little lip liner, little--" "No!" she cut me off. "We were very authentic and I would never wear make-up, playing a nun."

Should I have let it go? Yes. Did I let it go? No.

"Joan, easy. You're clearly wearing make-up in this shot." She said nothing and remained face down scrutinizing another image of herself from "The Sea Wife". "Ok...", I prodded, "I guess you're gonna make me get my loupe..." A loupe is a magnifying device used to examine photographs. "Do what you like," she said softly.

The room was packed with the boxes of photographs from her various films and publicity shoots. A little bit embarrassed for Joan, that I would have to go to such lengths, I rose from our work table, pushing numerous red library carts aside and crawling over the most magnificent black and white images of Joan when she was a contract player.

I emerged from my office, loupe in hand and proceeded toward our light boxes. "Ahem." I cleared my throat officiously and affixed one end of the loupe to my eye like a monocle, and the other to the light box, and bent over the transparency in question. While the loupe glided over her image like an Ouija Board, Joan said not a word. Finally, I sat up.

I sat tall in my chair, frustrated by the silence and lack of distractions. Not a stitch. Not a stitch of make-up that I could detect. Her natural coloring was incredible. I almost launched into that speech from "The Ten Commandments": something about "your skin, white as alabaster, your lips, red as rubies, your raven black bangs shimmer like the Nile." But I had learned to play it cool from the master who sat next to me. I sat quietly and finally I managed, "It *appears* that *perhaps* in this shot, you are not wearing any make-up." "Mmm," she said, half interested.

While the world believes Dame Joan Collins to be showy and big, I think her power comes in the quiet details. We know her as a two-dimensional tabloid cover, charged with yelling at bellhops somewhere. I don't doubt it, but there's so much more. She's benevolent and cleaver and quietly appealing. Who would have thought I would learn "less is more" from one of the biggest personalities in entertainment?

Academy Award winner and consummate showgirl Cloris Leachman came to my office at my behest. My dear friend, producer and staunch Malibu devotee, Cynthia Scrima offered the services of Cloris, as they had been pals for many years.

The archivists and I had been compiling images for a book Abrams would publish entitled *Twentieth Century Fox: Inside the Photo Archive*. We were supremely interested in the backstory of a shot from "Young Frankenstein" which found its way to page 50 of said book. The subject matter features Cloris whispering into Gene Wilder's ear as he crinkles with laughter. Desperate to know what she had whispered, we had lured Cloris to come in and take a look.

Cloris arrived with a battery of painful-sounding thuds at our door. The wet noses of two dogs pushed the door open and bounded in, pulling taught leashes, held firmly by Cloris. It looked like two dogs flying a movie star kite.

We screeched introductions. "What are your dogs' names?" I asked, enthusiastically. "Oh, it doesn't matter," Cloris said. And ya know, she was right. I remember their ample spirit and zest to this day, but would have never remembered their names.

"Could they get some water?", Cloris asked. "Of course!" I turned to one of the archivists and asked him to fill our cherished silver bowl with water. The archivist stopped in his tracks and looked at me with a wounded expression. The silver bowl was a key element in our five o'clock Friday ritual of cocktails in the Photo Archive. It was our ice bucket. Begrudgingly, he filled the bowl and the nameless dogs slopped away at it, with gusto.

As the dogs lounged, happily piled in the corner, Cloris took a seat at our library table. We placed the photograph before her. "Cloris Leachman," I began, "Do you recall your quip to Gene Wilder when this photo was taken?" She stared at it for a moment, looked down, slid her half-glasses from her face, and looked up at me. "How the hell would I remember what happened 30 years ago?!" The archivists and I were embarrassed for me.

For the next two hours we showed Cloris photographs, and she regaled us with stories one could only get from the source itself-- stories she *did*, in fact remember. She talked about her time with Eunice Kennedy, staying at the Shriver home when Maria was a little girl, and about making movies with Mel Brooks. I showed her a picture of the Fox lot under construction in 1926. "We were born the same year, this lot and me," she said. Cloris and the talkies were young together and they had grown up together.

At 20, Cloris had competed in the Miss America pageant, which perhaps served as a springboard to Hollywood. Nine Emmy Awards and an Academy Award later, she would find herself entertaining the archivists at Fox while her dogs slept beside her. Surrounded by people and animals who love you is not a bad place to be.

As I walked her to her car I got up the nerve to ask her if she remembered winning the Oscar. "No," she said, "I don't remember it at all," and she gave me a swift backhand smack across my chest, as if to say "Are you stupid?" She said she remembered picking out the dress, and the breathless anticipation of the evening, and like most winners, the moment it happened was somewhat of a blur. So maybe it wasn't such a dumb question after all. She asked me to dinner and I had to decline due to a prior commitment. Why didn't I break my dinner date?

Of anyone I've written about, Cloris is the most difficult to describe, but she is a heady thing. She left me light-headed, as if it was Christmas morning, or Lindbergh had just touched down in Paris. Cloris was 100% pure fun and I only wish I could get some more of her.

In 2006, ReganBooks was an imprint of HarperCollins Publishing, a sister company to Twentieth Century Fox under News Corp. Yes, the world is really run by approximately three people and one of them was Rupert Murdoch and his behemoth News Corp.

A year earlier, my 10-minute speech, introducing Fox's restored 70mm "Cleopatra" (1963) for the British Film Institute, was met with so much interest, I decided to make a book called *CLEOPATRA 1963*, that would chronicle the historic production, telling the story only in photographs, captioned with direct quotes from primary source participants.

Who better than ReganBooks' own Judith Regan, to partner with me in creating that book? I wrangled a meeting with Judith and her smart and preppily handsome colleague Cal Morgan who warned that she could be tough. Coupled with the current press on the popular Ms. Regan, I pictured "Sleeping Beauty's" Maleficent the Dragon, entering my office and just setting fire to whatever she hated, willy-nilly.

Judith was the publishing genius behind such books as Jenna Jameson's "How to Make Love Like a Porn Star" and her obvious coup de gras, yet to be distributed, *If I Did It*. The latter, O.J. Simpson's naughty, tee-hee of how he would have slain Nicole Brown Simpson and Ronald Goldman, escaping the Los Angeles County Criminal Court system, was met with disdain from the world public. An outcry of disgust snowballed from pre-release buzz, due to the book's tongue-in-cheek caginess and bad taste.

We all went mad for a while, in 1995, due to our obsession with a football hero. That madness was mirrored back to us in Judith's forthcoming book. It was all a bit too much, too soon. O.J. was so hot and sexy -- *plus* his acting was tolerable and he made so many tailgate parties a drunken dream as we sauntered out of the stadium, fat with potato salad and beer. Never mind that he slit Nicole's throat and held her body up to Ronald Goldman like a dead puppet before he stabbed Goldman to death, allegedly, or watched someone else do his dirty work (yet another theory), but we all knew he was part of it. I happened to be on jury duty during the O.J. trial, downtown. I rode the elevator with Forrest Whittaker and Magic Johnson and I too, got caught up in the magic. We all did. But it was a vile, filthy crime that could never be fit with a proper punishment. We leave him to God. Judith didn't kill anyone, however, and I may have published the book too, just as she did, printing 400,000 copies in 2006, waiting in a warehouse, ready to go.

Judith entered the Photo Archive wearing a starched white shirt and navy blazer. She probably completed the outfit with khaki trousers but in my mind, they were khaki jodhpurs and a riding crop. She was/is an attractive woman with a thick mane of brown hair cut bluntly at the shoulder blades and ready for business. I was petrified, but then slowly, I was taken by her childlike sense of wonderment at the room around her. Our main room was adorned with exceptional images from the Fox collection and her eyes darted around the pictures assimilating and judging, full of lust and grief and everything in between. I would not call Judith "judgy", but rather, highly opinionated, as I am, so, what a welcomed meeting it was.

By the end of our meeting I was literally on the floor of my office at her feet while she held a book in her lap. She was Cleopatra and I was a mere handmaiden, albeit a crabby, opinionated handmaiden, at her sandals. I was using the book she held as an example to demonstrate how I hated images that overlapped into the gutter at the book's fold. Photographs can be horribly obscured by as much as 10%, drowning in the stupid gutter.

I forget how, but by some means, film historian Eddie Muller, the "Czar of Noir" joined the meeting. Judith, Cal and Eddie whooped it up for the remaining 10 minutes until I noticed my archivists scampering about, zipping in and out of view through a square of glass cut in my office door. They bobbed up and down, shooting looks

72

into our meeting, all the while pretending not to. Dear God, what were they doing? Clearly something sinister was afoot.

Cal and Eddie bowed out leaving Judith and I to discuss next steps. I liked her a lot. We vowed to connect soon and she was off to her next appointment: a meeting with the Murdoch people across the studio's Avenue of the Palms, on the corporate side of the Fox lot. Fragments of the "Hello, Dolly!" parade set remained on *our* side of the Avenue but the corporate side had razed any remembrance of the "Dolly" parade scene to erect shiny new corporate headquarters of plastic and rubber. Their side of the Avenue was a sign of the times for any studio lot, like when Gulf+Western took over Paramount, affixing the name of oil maven Charles Bluhdorn to the building that supported Paramount Pictures' historic Bronson Gate.

I hate to write only nice things about people, but Judith was warm, personable, sensible, feminine, and only dipped a couple toes into the waters of "demonstrative". I was thrilled and relieved. The smart ones don't have to be evil. Surely she could be a tough cookie when required, as Jon Dolgen demonstrated at Paramount.

I'm reminded of a conversation I had with my good pal Gloria Miller, assistant to Rupert Murdoch after Murdoch came ambling past us through his office one day, smiling pleasantly. "Is he really *that* tough?" I asked. "Not at all! He's a pussycat," Gloria whispered, as she sorted his mail. "But in *business*," I pushed, "how is he in the *boardroom*?" Gloria stopped and shot her sparkling blue eyes over her half glasses, locking them with mine. "Ruthless," she said.

Off Judith Regan trapesed, as the Photo Archive door shut behind her.

The archivists began to squeal like a tribe of gnomes. "What is *wrong* with you?!" I charged. "She's fired!" they blurted. My head began to swim. I knew precisely what had happened: The archivists had read on the internet, of Judith's demise, which had been leaked to the press, even before her meeting ten minutes in the future, that would inform her of her own execution.

Judge me now, for not racing after Judith to tell her of her impending doom. Studio lore takes over here as I finish this essay telling you, Mr. Murdoch was not there to do the dirty work. He does run the world, after all, and he can't be present at every firing. Legend has it that Murdoch's henchperson Jane Freedman swung the axe. And Judith was let go, along with her triumphant ReganBooks, in the wake of the O.J. book scandal. What a shame, although I understand she got 10 large out of that clunky, off-putting dismissal.

I enjoyed Judith Regan and would still love to make that book with her. Maybe she'll read this and call me.

The lessons I learned in Hollywood were almost always about humility and survival. The best and most brutal example was learned while I was researching *CLEOPATRA 1963* for my talks abroad and the potential Judith Regan book project. Fox President Spyros Skouras, in 1958, had taken great pride in giving the production his personal greenlight approval, unaware of the legendary horror it would become.

The studio already owned the rights from their 1912, silent "Cleopatra" Theda Bara vehicle, and the world was mad for Elizabeth Taylor, her violet eyes begging to be framed in gallons of liquid eyeliner and breasts heaving under bolts of billowy 1963 chiffon.

Spyros had shepherded the project into the studio, the same way he herded flocks of sheep on the hillsides of Greece, as a boy with his trusty dog at his side, and crooked staff in hand as the clouds rolled by. Spyros could never imagine to be a part of Fox Film Corp's searchlights, flickering on his local cinema screen in his village, Skourochori. At 17, Skouras sailed for St. Louis, Missouri and made his way west, climbing the ladder with unbelievable success at Twentieth Century Fox, where he struck what seemed to be, the savvy Taylor-Burton deal.

Hollywood's contract studio system had come to an end and "Cleopatra" went into the meat grinder along with almost every facet of studio life, as they knew it. Studio life would emerge a Phoenix from the flames but Spyros would not. And the world looked on. A year in, the sheepherder whom half of Hollywood had slandered, was made to watch his livelihood spin down the drain. Plagued by a series of perfect storms, "Cleopatra" had become a runaway train—a financial and logistical monster, unstoppable. His baby had become a relentless killer like the monster in "Cloverfield". The shepherd boy was forced to watch it unfold on the cover of LIFE magazine and the Nightly News, enduring boundless humiliation as budgets spun out of control. His legacy would be the destruction of the industry he loved and built.

Darryl Zanuck took over as head of production. Movie colony tabloids hungered for that one great story—that one great shot of the shepherd boy's head rolling into a basket, but it never happened! Zanuck, in an uncharacteristic act of compassion, retained Skouras in an emeritus, figurehead position, stationed in an office down the hall from Zanuck in Bldg. 88.

Having little to do with making new movies, Skouras had changed. He bought a group of 7 oil tankers which he named the Prudential Line, and sometimes wore skipper hats to work. A bottle of Jim Beam in each coat pocket (ya can't fly on one wing), Skouras died 8 years after making "Cleopatra". What an unlikely ending to an otherwise brilliant career.

I know "profiling" is bad, but, oh well, here goes:

The Typical (But Not All) Bldg. 88 Girl Profile:

- *Tight black pants that flare above 3-inch chunky heels*
- *Breasts*
- *Edgy rectangular eyewear*
- *Pretty*
- *Nasally voice*
- *Mousy brown hair, slightly streaked with sexy pops of blonde, tortured hair by hair into a tortoise shell scrunchie so it looks like it was thrown together haphazardly after a night of sex.*

Nigel Arthur, the me of the British Film Institute, was working on a project on our lot one summer, when he heard the archivists and me speaking of the girls who worked in Bldg. 88.

Fox's Bldg. 88 was built in 1935 when Twentieth Century Pictures and Fox Film Corp merged. The 2-storey, football field-long structure is domicile to only those executives who make 6 or 7 figure salaries. If the hot, sexy assistants who work for those executives can bear the burden of that job, for more than, say, three years, the studio will typically set them up with a 2-year production deal.

So one balmy day as Nigel and I followed a murder of 88s, pecking their way to a late lunch of ginseng and sunflower seeds, the question was posed by Nigel: "Rob, what does it take to be a 'Bldg. 88 Girl'?" There is only one correct answer and it is two words. I stated it clearly for Nigel:

"Thick skin."

Nigel gave the British chuckle and said, "No, really. What sort of degree or training?" Brits can be amusing when they can't grasp the sincerity of our vile American ways, thinking we must be kidding. Fox 2000 Pictures' "The Devil Wears Prada" is an upbeat, smoothed-over cartoon of executive/assistant relationships. It is not "over the top", but rather an understated version of what goes on at the studio, and one presumes, in the fashion world. And just for the record, Anna Wintour is a dreamboat next to Darryl Zanuck or L.B. Mayer. You haven't *lived* until your studio exec boss shows his disapproval for a memorandum you've typed by calling you into his office, crumpling it into a ball while he stares you down, and tossing it at your feet. When you're made to get on all fours like a dog to pick up the memorandum, you come and talk to me about Meryl Streep throwing her purse on your desk. Please. But studio folk do not whine or complain (much). There simply isn't time for it.

Pain is temporary. Movies are forever.

Of all the stars in Hollywood and the heavens above, my favorite is Julie Andrews. Not because she's widely known and not because she's played likable characters, but just because she's Julie. If that sounds trite, then so be it. And if the public thinks honesty is trite then I am guilty as charged.

One wintry evening after dark, the story goes, Julie was scampering about the Fox lot with her manager Steve Sauer. He said "I want to show you something," and the pair knocked on the door of the Music Dept. Fox lifer Fran Block was working late and had the door to their bungalow suite locked. Fran crept toward the door, clutching her pearls, and in my mind, wearing curlers and a chenille robe. At the door stood the studio's benefactress and her manager/friend, staring through the three inches allowed by the door chain.

Let me be clear. Two people have saved Twentieth Century Fox from going belly up, and both are girls: Shirley Temple and Julie Andrews. Of course there was an army of heroes behind both of them, and of course Zanuck and Skouras and William Fox himself all play into the studio's enormous success, but not in such a specific, triumphant way. Without these two girls spearheading the juggernaut, the studio would have absolutely collapsed. That is not my opinion, but a fact.

Fran, after hours, had moved from a high-heeled shoe to a more comfortable fuzzy slipper-- also not my opinion, but a fact. She schlepped toward the door and screamed a little bit when she saw Julie and Steve. Fran opened the door with a welcoming but conservative flourish, maintaining a half-bow and shallow curtsey as they passed.

Steve pointed to an off-camera photograph that hung on the wall. There was Julie in 35mm black and white, working on "The Sound of Music". "I don't have that one," Julie noted and that's all Fran needed to hear. Fran told Ellen Ginsberg, and Ellen called me, and the Photo Archive was on it.

For the next several weeks I poured over the 50,000+ still photographs Fox retains from "The Sound of Music" production. I culled 90 images that I thought worthy of Julie, and had them printed in large format, hoping she might like a few.

Days later I straggled into work, late, hung over and repentant, cutting corners in an effort to escape as soon as possible until I got a call from Ellen Ginsberg at 1pm. "Grab the photos!" she yelled through the phone, "We're going to see Julie at the Beverly Wilshire Hotel!" "Awe, crap," I said. Ellen was calling from home on speaker, prancing about like a teen-age wood sprite, trying on different outfits, making a costume change out of her work attire. She went on to explain that she would be picking me up in 45 minutes. I snatched the photos, ran a toothless comb through my, gin-soaked hair and we were on our way to Wilshire and Rodeo where Julie was ensconced in a press junket for the release of "The Sound of Music" 40th Anniversary DVD.

Ellen and I bolted to the suite where the press junket was encamped. We didn't realize that two thirds of Julie was already present. John and Rick have been her stylists for many years, and they are family. The three of them present Julie to the media. When Julie stands, they stand too, as dutiful professionals, fixing hair, make-up and dress. It only takes a few seconds to be camera-ready, but critical to anyone of her stature. I wanted to take Rick and John home with me.

Julie entered and I shook her hand. Ever grab a lightning bolt? I was instantly reminded of cutting across a pasture as a child and touching an electric fence. "Hello," she said, looking me in the eye, earnest and calm, like a warm example from a self-assertiveness training class. She insisted I sit next to her and off we went.

The very best part of my job at Fox was meeting movie experts, whether it was a movie director, a secretary, a grip, or a star, and turning back the clock to a past we both somehow shared. I was blithely unaware as a child that going to the movies had been my homework for the future. If Spielberg thinks he directed "Jaws" alone, he's wrong. We were all there with him. And that goes for anyone making movies today. If they do their job well, we will all go back in time to learn everything we can about it, and we are caught up with them, spiritually, and completely equipped to reminisce as though we were there, physically.

Still photographers click away relentlessly every day on the set. To go through production stills is to relive the production experience, on-camera and off. Going down that path with Julie was no exception. There were so many memories fighting to be acknowledged. It is a rare phenomenon and apparent in Julie's eyes. Photographs are a visceral experience and our mind processes the information much faster than the story can be told, verbally. Emotions fly by too quickly to be spoken, but she was trying.

Speaking quickly and tapping her fingertips to her lips, her eyes darted around the subject matter. I chose images that I thought would be particularly personal for her. It's not possible to remember the names of everyone on a production crew, but in a better, more satisfying way, I think, those people could be felt in her heart as if it all happened yesterday. Still photographers on any movie set are geniuses at being invisible, with their zoom lenses and "blimps" to block any intrusive mechanical sounds. The off-camera images are often intimate and voyeuristic.

Julie and I were floating around Salzburg in 1964 at this point, and trapesing about the stages at Fox. She spoke fondly of Mark who gave her, her choreography. With equal affection, Julie pointed out her Music Director Saul Chaplin and the fastidious Dorothy Jeakins who designed Julie's costumes. We looked at images of the lecherous Viennese local who provided the cart and oxen that would transport Julie to that freezing meadow in the Alps. It all came alive for me. What a gift, to see it through her eyes. "Look at Bob," she said quietly, speaking of her director, Robert Wise. A shadowy image showed Bob wearing a somewhat wry expression while Julie stood before him in her stripped postulate attire, head down, listening intently. "Look at the coins," she said. "He was always fiddling with those coins to relieve

81

pressure or something." Yes, they could be seen in his up-turned hand. "The British pound, I'll bet," said I, "They're so fat it's hard *not* to play with them." She laughed and nodded.

We came to an image of Christopher Plummer. "What about Chris Plummer?" I pried. She looked heavenward, "Delicious," she said. That answered that. She pointed out little Duane, who played one of the Von Trapp children, seen in our photos placing daisies in her hair. "He was my favorite", she said.

As afternoon turned to evening, someone asked me if I wanted a drink. They probably meant lemonade, but having such a good time I called out "Tanqueray and tonic". "Martini", Julie chimed in, as it was indeed 5 o'clock. A message came from Julie's husband Blake Edwards. "Blake is waiting at Trader Vic's", Steve Sauer relayed. "Tell Blackie to wait—I'm having too much fun with Rob," Julie trilled. Of course she didn't mean it, as we wrapped in ten minutes, but I was thrilled that she would pretend to put me before her Hollywood icon husband Blake Edwards!

Feeling cheeky, I said to Julie, "Just go with me on this: you're 15 or so, planted in the audience at the Palladium in London's West End, poised to take the stage. What was going through your mind?" Surely she had told the story a hundred times, but she took her time with me. "The bit was to call a random girl from the audience. I was dressed all in white. I approached the stage nervously to sing, and, well…" "And you blew the lid off the Palladium," I said. Julie smiled a broad grin and said, 'That was that, and I never looked back."

Someone handed her something to sign and people began to hover around her. "Whoa, whoa, whoa…," I said, "What do you mean?" "My career had begun," she answered, "Everything changed, in that moment. There was no going back."

As we stood to say good-bye, we engaged in that bizarre ritual that my mother used to succumb to when her guests left her Bridge parties: the 10-minute chit-chat toward the door. Julie stopped in the middle of a story about her experience taping the live televised "Cinderella" in which she starred. At a loss for a moment, she asked, "Who was it who played my step-sister?" I offered: "Kaye Ballard". "That's it, Rob!" and we jumped up and down like game show winners. I was so excited that I got it right!

The next time Julie and I met was at Blake Edwards' art show at the Pacific Design Center. Unbeknownst to most of the world, Blake was an incredible painter and sculptor. I think it's hard for people to get their minds around the fact that Blake could be a great movie director, *and* sculptor *and* painter, but he was. When someone is loaded with that much talent, I don't believe there's time for him, or us to fully appreciate the scope of his being. Most of us think of Blake as a handsome silvery-haired funny guy, but in his 20s, and beyond, he was physically, very beautiful. That alone would keep most of us busy for a lifetime in Los Angeles.

At that event I waited patiently to approach Julie because there is always a crowd of well-wishers surrounding her, about 10 deep. I've always imagined that from the air, any Julie Andrews event must look like a Wi-Fi symbol with Julie at the hub and the crowd emanating from her like a fan.

My friend Dean was with me, half-listening to an incredible string quartet employed for the event, and suddenly we saw Julie put her arm around a distinguished looking man. He and Julie turned toward the press as flashbulbs popped. "We haven't done this in a long time", said Julie to the man, in a way that felt warm and fuzzy. She put her head on the man's shoulder and the flashing continued.

The man left her side and I moved in. I could not place that man's face. "Who was that?" I asked. "That was Army!" she said, "Army Archerd". I became light-headed, and managed "Whaaat?!" Army's daily column, *Just for Variety* was a part of my physical make up for years. Clock alarm, shower, coffee and Army were critical to my living each day. "I love him!", I cried. "Rob, you need to tell him," said Julie,

"He's semi-retired and only does his column occasionally now. And he's getting away!" We turned quickly in his direction. At the far end of the Pacific Design Center concourse, Army and his wife could be seen climbing into their limo.

I cannot believe I dropped Julie's hand—hey, when it rains, it pours— and sprinted through 10 different perfumes, 100 cocktails and the exceptional string quartet across the super-glossy floor of the PDC. I waved my hands above my head at the limo and, Army, just getting in, turned and stepped out. "Army," I gushed (and I do mean gushed), "Julie said-- I mean I told Julie, and she, we saw you leaving, and, you are a part of my life, and I couldn't have… ya know…" Army chuckled, knowingly; the fiber of so many Tinsel Town lives, as he shook my hand. His wife, with the cutest blonde upturned haircut ever, smiled from across the top of the car.

Who else but Army could come up with fake correspondents like his London tattler "Tiana Crumpet" or his local sidekick "Onda Lotalot"? Hollywood hung on their every word for so many years, as we the readers, flung open page one of Daily Variety.

When I told Army I worked in the Archives at Fox, he asked if I could find a screen test he made in the 40's. He had tested at Fox with a tall actress but couldn't recall her name. I set to work on it the following Monday, but the studio wheels grind slowly. Before we could produce that screen test from our Film Library, Army was gone. I hate good-byes and won't dwell on it here, except to say he gave me a reason to get up in the morning. How do you quantify that? To me he was invaluable and peerless. I am grateful to Julie for pointing me in his direction that night.

Another good-bye came much too soon when Julie lost her Blake Edwards. The farewell tribute to Blake at the Director's Guild in 2011 was more than spectacular. Parking was free which meant it was going to be a magical night. Dean and I noted that everyone there was famous but us, and once again, Julie was a Wi-Fi logo with crowds fanning out from her at its hub, wanting to give he. love. I turned to a marauding server to snatch a pizza popper from the tray, when I was met by two other grabbers. Helen Mirren and Debbie Reynolds would have to fight it out for themselves as my arm recoiled in reverence.

Speaking of Debbie, she sat in front of me in the auditorium where we reveled in clips from Blake's films. She asked me to retrieve her program as she had kicked it under her seat. As she turned, smiling up at me, I leaned in, scrutinizing every line I could find on her face. The actress looked 35, and I'm not saying that to be nice-- had I known better, I would have circus side-show guessed her age at 35. I fantasized about dumping out the contents of her purse and stealing the card of her doctor for future reference. She looked *fantastic*.

The original clarinet player from Blake's Pink Panther movies played the panther theme with its sneaky cat-like sex appeal. A combo was on hand to accompany a gorgeous rendition of "Moon River" sung by Melissa Manchester, to commemorate what I would say is Blake's best loved film, "Breakfast at Tiffany's". We heard from others associated with Blake's achievements that include "My Sister Eileen", "The Great Race" and "Victor/Victoria" to name a few. What a champ for movie making he was. The forever-beautiful Bo Derek spoke about how Blake had launched her career in "10".

Ted Chapin, a wonderful author and head of the Rogers & Hammerstein Organization came to the Photo Archive one day to look over stills for the upcoming "The Sound of Music" DVD and Blu-ray releases. I had him sign my copy of the book he authored called "Everything Was Possible" about his college internship as Stephen Sondheim and Hal Prince's assistant when they were creating the musical "Follies". I understand you've met with Julie", Ted said. "Yes," I answered, nervously aware of where he was going with his comment. "Ya know," Ted went on, "not many people get an audience with Julie." "Really?" I asked, rhetorically. "Really", he said. And somehow I knew it was true. Not that Ted couldn't get her at a moment's notice, but still, he regarded me suspiciously and with a glint in his eye that suggested, "Good for you".

Weeks later I stood outside a screening room at Fox waiting to go over some photos with Julie, and I got the call that my best friend had tried to kill himself. I flung the box of photos to a secretary and ran for my car. I do have priorities once in a while, sort of. I did, however, lecture and scold my suicidal pal relentlessly, not for overdosing on anti-freeze, but for making me miss Julie!

Months later I was able to beg Steve Sauer for another meeting, and I came to Julie in Santa Monica where she was entertaining the press at a beautiful hotel overlooking the Pacific Ocean. I crept into her suite with the box of photos under my arm—sumptuous images of Julie from "Star!".

As I entered, I heard Julie call, "Rob, is that you?" "Well it ain't Chris Plummer," I answered back, unsure of what I meant, myself, although I thought it sounded quippy and show-bizzy.

Julie and Steve and an army of peeps greeted me warmly. Although I had forced this meeting that could have been handled by phone and courier, I lapped it up and felt a certain level of comfort, finally, however pushed, with the gal Ted Chapin called "tough to get". While going over the color prints from "Star!", Julie paused and remarked, "This shot of me was used on the cover of one of my biographies." "Did you read it?" I asked. "Oh, no," she said, kindly, not sure if I was kidding or not, and the room bubbled with soft chuckles at my silly question.

If someone had written my biography, I would have dissected every syllable and supervised a marketing blitz with amazon. That's why Julie lives successfully in that world, where people are typically the subject of biographies, and I do not.

While Julie's gifts as an artist and a performer are a thrill for any audience, her ability to understand and navigate fame is equally brilliant. It may be her greatest gift, and most people never see her natural strategy in action. When meeting with her, for example, one might come away remembering a lovely afternoon where ideas were exchanged and goals were set. One could swear they had a meeting with Julie, but she actually resides on a different planet. With a completely different set of concerns, building and navigating fame, she lives on Jupiter and I live on Saturn. And once in a while, we orbit so that our worlds come close enough to wave hello across the galaxy.

There isn't a patented formula or manual for achieving popularity or fame. There is no recipe for charisma. Most theories agree that certain elements must be in play: talent, ambition, geography, luck, and she has connected the dots.

So many people want to know her or want to befriend her. Again, it's not because she's widely known and plays likable parts. It's because she's Julie and great at being Julie. Sorry, England. She is not only ours, but also, our national treasure.

With Julie at the Beverly Wilshire Hotel, 2005.

My dear friend Penny Nickels phoned one day to catch up and tell me she had been employed as Reba McEntire's stand-in on the hit TV show "Reba". Both Penny and Reba had flaming red hair so I was not surprised.

Reba, an incredible vocal anomaly and beloved country storyteller through song, had found her way into the hearts of America, even more so, through her television show, shot just across the parking lot from me at Fox. Over the next few weeks, Penny regaled me with Reba stories and hilarious anecdotes to send this boy from Eugene, Oregon, reeling.

One afternoon during camera blocking, Penny found herself next to the nurturing and maternal Reba while dishing up pasta, via Craft Services on the set. Reba couldn't help but notice, Penny told me, that Penny's hands were chafed and dry. "Flaxidol", Reba whispered into Penny's ear, shooting glances at Penny's rough-hewn claws. "What?" Penny pretended. "Flaxidol," Reba repeated. No longer able to pretend, Penny said, "Oh, for my dry hands, you mean?" Reba shook her head yes. Penny of course scurried to write down the mysterious drug so she could ask her doctor for a prescription. An omnipresent stage manager saw the entire exchange, including Penny's quick jotting of the drug. "Penny, you do know what Reba said, don't you?" Penny stared at him for an answer. "Flax seed oil," the stage manager, said. Penny was thrilled and relieved that Reba had an interpreter.

When I completed my photo book for Fox that I've already plugged to death in this volume, Penny and I cooked up a scheme. Mind you, I had delivered the Fox photo book to movie stars and dignitaries at the request of the company, but I WANTED REBA! I am an insufferable Reba fan. Who can hear "Starting Over Again" without weeping? Penny suggested I present the book to her on behalf of the studio. "'Reba' set, Tuesday morning", Penny lured.

In my inscription, I gave Miss Reba a benevolent and fatherly welcome to the Fox family, citing her penchant for the still image. I offered our little collection of bound images with love. I strode onto the "Reba" stage, book under one arm and began to show grips and production staff my tome while Penny sent for the star, then in make-up.

As I entertained the troops, issuing quips about this photo and that, I noticed a diminutive person approaching from the far end of the vast stage. The figure was about 3 feet tall, wore her hair in an orange flip that framed a blank orange face. As Reba purposefully and with a somewhat bitter sense of determination, placed one flat Angel Tread slipper in front of the other to reach us, I could tell she was not a happy camper—m-kay?

What to do, what to do? Clearly I am not an expert at most things. I cannot cook or work on cars or sing or—well, you name it, I can't do it. But I am good in crisis. As Reba approached, I was taken with her natural, youthful appearance. As I said, she had only undergone a base coat of make-up—no eyes, no lips, no contouring, and she looked 17.

"You must be Reba McEntire's daughter!" I said, extending my hand. "Wha—oh-- well!" said the tiny songstress. "I have the biggest mouth on this lot," I went on, "and I am going to tell everyone you look like a teenager." "Whatever you say", she grinned. Reba really did look incredible. I couldn't believe it.

Penny Nickels and I began the self-created presentation, supposedly engineered by the company. "Well, Reba," Penny began, "Rob, here, has written a book, and, well, go ahead, Rob…" "That's right, Reba," I went on, "I… *we*… wanted you to have this book, because we know you are a fan of the still image, and because you are now part of our Fox family, and well, because we all love you—we all love you more than—more than Christmas morning!" Penny shot me a look as if to say the last part was going too far. "That's real cute," Reba said, sincerely. "Where did you get that line?". "From me", I said. Reba smiled as she looked back and forth, from me to the book while

The Dream

Like DeNiro playing a crunchy Italian or James Coburn wearing a sexy, womanizing turtleneck, some things are a perfect fit. Audience members are stuck with those visceral moments that later trigger memories. It all becomes very personal and, in fact, it becomes the fabric of our lives.

In movie-making, there are unknown variables and equations that defy explanation but are key to its success. Capturing these elusive elements within stories on film, is a lesson in the art of patience for a brutally impatient business.

A moment of transcendence which allows the dream to take over and communicate with its audience is the result of true inspiration and it is the heart of cinema. We use terms like "movie magic" and "star power" to describe the experience. Clara Bow was simply "It". The end result is measured by an emotional response and scientific explanation is inconsequential.

To be part of the movies was always my dream. I only ever wanted to work in the movies and I became part of it, firmly planted in the American landscape.

It is not so much America, but rather, the American ideal that will raise you up. We continue to share the dream of movies with the world, because it is the most we have to give.

After seven years of begging any laborer I met, or anyone with a hammer swinging from a loop on their grubby cargo shorts, I was finally awarded an invitation to the Fox Grip Christmas Party and it was so worth the wait.

At Paramount I befriended the Sign Shop gang. I was honored with my name in cream colored script, painted indelibly on my studio-sanctioned purple bicycle. *"Rob"*, it said, with the weird quotation marks around it.

When presented to me, I knew I was one of them. It's such a small thing and yet, I had been made part of a rich history. I knew what producer Robert Evans felt when he returned to the lot after being dragged away by Security, years earlier. Never mind that Bob had brought "Chinatown" and "The Godfather" to the screen, as one of Paramount's hardest working producers. Upon Bob's return, a gardener from the Greens Dept. pulled out Robert's signature, forged in thick brass. The gardener polished it and reattached it to Bob's outdoor shingle. The gardener had saved it for him, and what a meaningful homecoming it was for the Prodigal Son. In our little movie colony, those moments of acceptance mean everything.

There is a vicious and time-honored tradition among studio folk, of bicycle stealing. I was victim to it, and perhaps it's all part of that rite of passage. After one year, my purple bike was gone, but I dream about it. I was 26 and my name was on it and I felt I was somebody. I felt I had arrived.

I dream about it at night, and in my dreams I am pedaling by the Dressing Room Bldg. at the 'mount. I peel around Stage 5 and up into the sky over Brooklyn Street and the Bronx Zoo set. I'm flying on my bike, above the lot, waving to studio pals who are going about their insular studio life and I feel like the kid from "E.T.", pedaling and coasting, solidly anchored by the purple bike beneath me.

CPSIA information can be obtained
at www.ICGtesting.com
Printed in the USA
LVHW111647241120
672600LV00020B/110/J

9 781480 891418